IMPLEMENTING A CRITICAL APPROACH TO ORGANIZATION DEVELOPMENT

The Professional Practices in Adult Education and Lifelong Learning Series explores issues and concerns of practitioners who work in the broad range of settings in adult and coutinuing education and lifelong learning.

The books provide information and strategies on how to make practice more effective for professionals and those they serve. They are written from a practical viewpoint and provide a forum for instructors, administrators, policy makers, counselors, trainers, instructional designers, and other related professionals. The series contains single author or coauthored books only and does not include edited volumes.

Sharan B. Merriam
Ronald M. Cervero
Series Editors

IMPLEMENTING A CRITICAL APPROACH TO ORGANIZATION DEVELOPMENT

Laura L. Bierema
University of Georgia

KRIEGER PUBLISHING COMPANY
MALABAR, FLORIDA
2010

Original Edition 2010

Printed and Published by
KRIEGER PUBLISHING COMPANY
KRIEGER DRIVE
MALABAR, FLORIDA 32950

Library of Congress Cataloging-in-Publication Data

Bierema, Laura L. (Laura Lee), 1964-
 Implementing a critical approach to organization development / Laura
L. Bierema. — Original ed.
    p. cm. — (The professional practices in adult education and lifelong
learning series)
 Includes bibliographical references and index.
 ISBN-13: 978-1-57524-266-8 (alk. paper)
 ISBN-10: 1-57524-266-4 (alk. paper)
 1. Organizational change. I. Title.
 HD58.8.B513 2010
  658.4'06—dc22

                                                          2009040722

10 9 8 7 6 5 4 3 2

To Mark Ebell

CONTENTS

PREFACE

Organizations are characterized by the constancy of and the inability to cope with change. The field of organization development (OD) provides proven strategies to help organizations plan change as well as respond to unplanned change at individual, group, and system levels. As a human resource developer or adult educator, you are often at the center of planning, implementing, and evaluating change. Not only are you responsible for instigating timely, effective, and lasting change, but also you are in the tenuous position of responding to employee and organization needs which are not always compatible. You also have the challenge of conducting your work in a way that is consistent with your values and protective of your political standing. There is a need for an organization development book that addresses these paradoxes and offers solutions for attending to competing needs and clashing interests effectively and democratically. Typical organization development and change strategies tend to glaze over contested issues of power and interests and may ignore issues related to social justice. Therefore, there is a need for a book that addresses principles and strategies for implementing a critical approach to organization development.

Organization development has many influences including organization behavior, management, psychology, sociology, economics, systems theory, and education. The unique perspective you bring as a human resource development (HRD) professional or adult educator is a commitment to growth and development, combined with an understanding of learning and change; values that are compatible with OD's core values. Additionally, the HRD perspective brings tools and techniques for developing human and organization potential on individual, group, and system levels, while the adult education perspective brings a commitment to social justice and knowledge of learning and development. Throughout my career I have melded the best HRD and adult education has to offer and believe these fields can make a special contribution to creating a more holistic, critical OD practice. I believe that contemporary HRD has strayed from OD's values of humanism and sustainable change in favor of enhancing human performance (performativity: the unrelenting pursuit of performance and profit above all else), subsequently advancing organization profit. There is a need for a book that frankly discusses the contradictory nature of developing individuals and organizations simultaneously, that challenges HRD to reconnect with the roots and values of OD and embrace the values of adult education. There is great potential for these fields to fuse together techniques and philosophy in a manner that can better meet the challenges of a hurting world.

As long as I have been in these two fields, adult education has pitted itself against HRD, accusing it of unbridled capitalism and opportunism. Setting up false binaries hurts both fields of practice and their practitioners. It is not productive for adult education to diminish the contributions to the understanding of learning in organization contexts that have been generated by the field of HRD, nor is it wise for HRD practitioners to ignore issues of social justice, power, and development that are so prominent in adult education. It is my goal to merge the contributions of HRD and adult education in a framework for conducting OD that is responsible, democratic, and sustainable.

It is beyond the scope of this book to settle once and for all the differences between adult education and HRD, yet I assert that perpetuating this separation creates an artificial binary that is not realized in practice, nor is it constructive for the many students of adult education who find themselves in contradictory organization structures and situations where they must be effective, ethical agents of multiple stakeholders. It also means that HRD may not benefit from the practices and perspectives of adult education.

This book attempts to draw on the best of adult education and HRD theory and technique to show how effective these fields can be when combined to address organization challenges in innovative and ethical ways. As a practitioner, I have found it both impossible and impractical to separate these two fields. They inform and enrich my practice in myriad ways.

In particular, adult education contributes to our understanding of organizations through its dedication to social justice; understanding of adult development learning and change; advancing individual, social, and critical analysis; and commitment to diversity and multicultural education. HRD also makes practical and theoretical contributions in the areas of change, career development, training, organization development, strategic leadership, and organization analysis and diagnosis, and interventions on levels ranging from the individual to the system.

Change is very difficult when it is forced or disrespectful of stakeholders. This book will analyze the organization development and change process, address the contradictory nature of facilitating organization development, critique OD practices that are undertaken without concern for development, growth, or stakeholders, and provide strategies and theoretical justification for conducting *developmental and sustainable* organization development and change. The book will be built around an alternative model and framework of OD and offer examples of how you can integrate critical principles into your own practice.

PURPOSE

The purpose of this book is to provide an introduction to organization development theory and practice for human resource developers and adult educators. It provides definitions, competencies, a framework, exhibits, and strategies on individual, group, and system levels. This book takes a critical approach to analyzing organization development and change, and addresses the inherent challenges in mitigating competing interests in the process. Rather than approaching organization issues neutrally, this book takes a perspective that the world is in trouble and our current organization practices are creating more debt, exploiting workers, disenfranchising marginalized groups, polluting the world, exploiting natural resources, perpetuating wars, and deepening poverty. I am impatient with the lack of progress we are making to address social ills using current approaches. Those of us who are doing developmental work have a large responsibility for challenging the system and using our talents to make the world a better place. We cannot wait for other practitioners, professions, or organizations to do this important work for us.

This book does not address every aspect of OD and change theory or all possible interventions. Good traditional supplements include *Organization Development and Change* by Cummings and Worley (2005), *Organization Development* by French and Bell (1999), *Organization Development* by McLean (2006), and *Organization Change* by Burke (2008).

CRITICAL ACTION RESEARCH MODEL

Action research, a widely used framework for OD, is a cyclical process that alternates between action and reflection in problem solving. Action research usually involves those affected by the change in an iterative process of data collection, decision making, implementation, and evaluation. The model in this book explains how to implement an action research model that has a critical dimension. In theory, action research is supposed to be critically reflective and egalitarian. In reality, this step has been diluted in OD literature and practice and compounded by pressure for OD to cater exclusively to management interests. This book will bring critical reflection to the forefront of OD, strengthen the bridge between adult education and HRD, and task us as OD consultants to be more critical and reflective.

The theoretical framework of this book's Critical Action Research Model draws on critical management studies (Alvesson & Deetz, 2000; Alvesson & Willmott, 1996), feminist theory (Bierema, 2002; Martin, 2003), critical human resource development (Bierema & Fenwick, 2005; 2008), critical cultural studies (Fenwick, 2000; Kellner, 1995), and a critical-interpretive approach (Alvesson, 1996; Deetz & Kersten, 1983). Each thread will be briefly described.

Critical management studies (CMS) seeks to foster insight, provide critique, and create a "transformative redefinition" of organization practices, cultures, and structures (Alvesson & Deetz, 2000). Critical theory informs CMS's effort to "challenge the legitimacy and counter the development of oppressive institutions and practices" (Alvesson & Willmott, 1996, p. 13) and its vision is to emancipate workers and create more accountability for managers whose acts impact the lives of employees and other stakeholders (Alvesson & Willmott, 1996). CMS has been criticized for having a significant disconnect between theory and practice. This book uses CMS principles as a springboard for conceptualizing a critical organization development framework.

Feminist theory seeks to expose both obvious and subtle gender inequalities, as well as critique patriarchal hegemony (Martin, 2003). Feminists work to change the asymmetrical power relationships in organizations and society and acknowledge that organizations are patriarchal and are generally structured to benefit white males in their policies and practices. Feminists recognize the sexist nature of organizations and aim to change it. The Critical Action Research Model presented in this book draws on Tisdell's (1995) work defining poststructural feminist theories and recognizing experience in context as affected by interlocking positionalities including race, class, and gender. Although feminism emerged to address women's inequality in society, it is equally concerned with addressing inequalities of other groups in society including ethnic, racial, and sexual minorities. To that end, this book aims to emphasize concerns of marginalized populations when planning and making OD interventions with the goal of democratic OD. Several examples throughout the book relate to gender and diversity, drawing on critical and feminist principles.

Critical human resource development seeks to apply CMS principles to HRD. In comparison to CMS, critical HRD is relatively underdeveloped. It is discussed in the literature (Elliott & Turnbull, 2002; Fenwick, 2000), yet the human resource development (HRD) field has not widely embraced critical principles (neither has management). It is not discussed in the major HRD textbooks and Elliot and Turnbull (2002) are concerned "that the methodological traditions that guide the majority of HRD research do not allow researchers to engage in studies that challenge the predominately performative and learning-outcome focus of the HRD field" (p. 971). They make a plea to open HRD theory to broader perspectives, yet within HRD this appeal has fallen on deaf ears. I define critical

HRD as: Critical human resource development challenges the concept of a performative HRD practice arguing for a critical and socially conscious HRD that problematizes its precepts by challenging the commodification of employees, involving multiple
stakeholders, contesting the nature of power relations, pursuing wide-
ranging goals (not just profit), while providing alternative, non-op-
pressive, holistic models for cultivating development in work context. The book will show how to apply critical principles to
implementing HRD practices given the field's focus on training and
development, career development, and organization development.

Critical cultural analysis has been recommended as an alternative conceptual frame for understanding and practicing HRD. This
approach critically "analyze[s] the structures of dominance that ex-
press or govern the workplace's social relationships, its communication forms, and its cultural practices" (Fenwick, 2000, p. 303).
This approach can help counter the lack of attention given to issues
of power common in the systems approach of many OD models.
CCA draws on diverse influences including: gender, ideology and
discourse analysis, media analysis, postcolonialism studies, queer
theory, race and identity, and technoculture theory (Fenwick, 2000).
Fenwick describes applications for this framework including: situat-
ing organization cultural sites in historical context, recognizing visible and dominant discourses in the culture, identifying prominent
representations of people within the cultural texts (i.e., managerial
rationality and neutrality as the norm), distinguishing organizational
boundaries that control the workplace culture, differentiating what
pieces of culture have interest and meaning for particular groups in
the culture (i.e., ethics, empowerment practices), and identifying what
patterns of colonialism are operating in the culture.

The critical-interpretive approach described by Alvesson
(1996), and Deetz and Kersten (1983) reconceptualizes the action
research model. A critical-interpretive approach involves understanding, critiquing, and learning. Understanding requires developing
awareness that organization conditions are not composed of unchanging structures devoid of human influence, nor are they objective and rational. Instead, organization conditions are human creations that are mutable. In this model, *understanding* incorporates
the action research steps of contracting, defining organization reali-

ties, and collecting and analyzing data. The second step of a criti-cal-interpretive approach involves critique. *Critique* recognizes that organizations are socially constructed and value-laden reflecting asymmetrical power relations and competing interests. Critique in this model will involve conducting a cultural analysis, identifying interests and values, and acknowledging power asymmetries. The *learning* phase involves creating meaningful change building upon understanding and critique. In this model, learning incorporates in-terpreting the understanding and critique steps, determining and implementing action, and critically evaluating the results. This is similar to an action learning approach with iterative cycles of action and reflection.

CONTRIBUTION

Most OD books are written from a management perspective that assumes management, and therefore OD practice, is a rational, neutral process. Further, these books tend to favor performative val-ues and align with management interests, within a corporate con-text. This book's key departure from existing texts is its application of a Critical Action Research Model that advocates representative, responsible, and reflective OD practice. It is *representative* in that it considers a broad range of stakeholders in the OD process and is-sues that are relevant to them. It also adds a developmental perspec-tive and broadens the context of OD beyond the corporate sector to include nonprofit organizations, government, healthcare, and edu-cation institutions. It is *responsible* in that it engages in rigorous attempts to understand and critique organization phenomena with a long term goal of social justice and democratic OD practice. It is *reflective* in that it engenders learning and follows a critical action research and action learning process to help maximize learning and development from OD endeavors.

INTENDED AUDIENCE

This book will be of interest to practitioners of organization development and change, particularly in HRD and adult education. The book is intended to raise issues related to social justice and democratic OD that have been ignored in traditional texts, making this book of interest to those working for social justice and change. The book is written in a style that is accessible to a wide range of people doing organization development and change work in a variety of settings.

USES

This book will be useful to the practitioner who is seeking to understand the theory behind practice, improve practice, critique practice, and evaluate practice. Each chapter offers practical strategies. This book will also prove useful in university courses on organizations, change, administration, management, and human resource development.

STRUCTURE OF THE BOOK

The book contains seven chapters. Chapter 1 provides a historical account of OD's emergence and tracks key interventions that have shaped it from its beginnings in the 1940s to the present day. Chapter 2 defines OD and introduces the book's critical framework and action research model. Chapter 3 introduces the critical OD consultant and examines core competencies. Chapter 4 identifies the stakeholders in the OD process and advocates a socially responsible OD practice. Chapter 5 addresses the context of OD and examines how a contested, multicultural, and complex environment shapes OD. Chapter 6 introduces critical OD interventions. The book concludes with Chapter 7 that reflects on how to create a representative, relevant, reflective, and responsible OD through the implementation of critical OD principles and interventions.

ACKNOWLEDGMENTS

A number of people have contributed their time and knowledge to the writing of this book. To the University of Georgia Human Resource and Organization Development graduate students, who read and offered comments on earlier drafts of the book and to UGA masters and doctoral students Gigi Burke Carr, Monica Cannon, Nan Fowler, and Kelly Sorensen who helped with research, proofreading, and intervention identification, I thank you for editing draft chapters, tracking down references, and identifying potential interventions. To UGA Ph.D. students, Tonya Cornelius and Selena Blankenship, who helped me co-teach a course using draft chapters, I thank you for your wisdom and feedback on the book and framework. I am also indebted to my colleagues and Krieger Series editors Ronald M. Cervero and Sharan B. Merriam, both of the University of Georgia, who critiqued the book's organization and draft chapters and provided invaluable direction in the development of the book. I am also grateful to editor Mary Roberts who provided outstanding feedback and editing suggestions that strengthened the book. Finally, the book would not be written without the unwavering support of my spouse, Mark Ebell, who endured the absences and anxieties associated with writing this book.

THE AUTHOR

Laura L. Bierema is professor of adult education and human resource development at the University of Georgia, Athens, Georgia. She received her B.A. degree (1986) in human relations from Michigan State University, her M.L.I.R. (masters of labor & industrial relations) (1988) from Michigan State University, and her Ed.D. degree (1994) in adult education from the University of Georgia. Before coming to the University of Georgia, she served on the faculties of Michigan State University and Washtenaw Community College. Prior to her career in academia, Bierema held a number of human resource and organization development positions in the automotive industry.

Bierema's research and writing activities have focused on creating a critical human resource development stream of research and practice, exploring women's learning and development in the workplace, and incorporating a feminist analysis to HRD discourse, research, and praxis. She has been involved with the Academy of Human Resource Development (AHRD) since its inception, currently serving on the board and as vice president for research. She is the first track editor of AHRD's "Critical HRD and Social Justice Perspectives" research track and also helped found and currently chairs the AHRD special interest group in critical HRD. She has been recognized by AHRD with four "Cutting Edge" awards recognizing the 10 best conference papers at each annual conference. She is also the recipient of the AHRD Richard A. Swanson Award for Excellence in Research. Bierema is a former co-editor of *Adult Education Quarterly* and has served on the editorial board of that journal, *Human Resource Development Quarterly,* and *Vocations and Learning.* Her other books include *Philosophy and Practice of Organizational Learning, Performance, and Change* (2001, coauthored with J. W. Gilley and P. Dean), *Critical Issues in Human Resource Development* (2003, co-edited with A. M. Gilley and J. Callahan), and *Women's Career Development across the Lifespan: Insights and Strategies for Women, Organizations and Adult Educators* (1998).

CHAPTER 1

The Rise and Evolution of Organization Development

Change is a constant in life that may be intended or unexpected, consensus-driven or directed, welcome or unwelcome, resisted or embraced, celebrated or berated, or met with dozens of other reactions. Organization development (OD) is an applied field created to facilitate planned change in organizations. Yet, it also should be concerned with maintaining stability or balance (Tannenbaum in Wheatley, Tannenbaum, Griffin, & Quade, 2003). OD emerged in the mid-20th century to create systems of culture change distinct from prevailing management development and human relations training at the time (Beckhard, 1997).

Organizations and the individuals who work in them face continual challenges as they grapple with the dizzying pace of change that requires quick responses. These challenges include globalizing markets, managing knowledge, diversifying workforces, and advancing technology. There are significant global costs to the shifting markets and growing economies that are creating poverty and environmental destruction. We now live in a world where the wealth of the 200 richest people exceeds the combined annual income of the world's 2.5 billion poorest people (Senge Smith, Kruschwitz, Laur, & Schley, 2008). Nearly half the world lives on $2 per day as compared to $130 per day for average Americans (Senge et al., 2008). The United States is a wasteful nation creating approximately 1 ton of waste per person per day (Senge et al., 2008). Senge et al. also note that globalization has brought unprecedented interdependence between nations, as well as problems such as environmental crises, eroding finite natural resources, and global terrorism. Yet, in the face of the obvious need to change, most people get busy trying to preserve the status quo.

Most of us will spend one-third of our lives working in organizations (Goldman Schuler, 2004a), giving them significant influence in our lives and underscoring the importance of assuring organizations are healthy places. Senge et al. (2008) suggest that for-profit business is the most influential institution in society, making it imperative to look to these organizations for participation in and solutions to world crises. Many organizations rely on professionals known as organization development consultants to steer them through these complex and shifting environments. OD consultants are competent observers of human behavior, authentic communicators with their clients, and adept influencers of change processes. Senge et al. also recommend that fundamental change requires seeing systems, collaborating across boundaries, and creating desired futures, key responsibilities of the OD professional.

This book advocates that OD consultants also are stewards of social justice and a democratic OD process. Organization development takes a long view of change, applying systems-based interventions on multiple levels to help individuals, groups, the organization, and sometimes broader constituents function more effectively. This chapter offers a definition of OD and briefly covers OD history and philosophy, identifies its core values, and raises critiques.

OD'S CORE VALUES AND PHILOSOPHY

Most of us want to do meaningful work in an organization that is pleasant to work in, with colleagues who are respectful, and an organization that recognizes and rewards our work. OD has sought to improve workplaces and the individual and group that populate them from its inception. A distinguishing feature of OD is its humanistic value system that aims to do no harm, build individual and system capacity, and uphold values of responsibility and sustainability. "The OD value is not about change but about change that makes people better—humanistic values" (Marshak in Wheatley, Tannenbaum, Griffin, & Quade, 2003, p. 4). OD's early focus favored individual development causing some scholars to call for putting the "O" back into OD (Beckhard in Porras & Bradford, 2004), with a renewed commitment to an organization focus. Today, OD seeks balance between honoring the individual while simultaneously advancing organization goals. OD experts across the board would argue that OD's humanistic values are critical to the field (Greiner & Cummings, 2004; Porras & Bradford, 2004; Wirtenberg et al., 2004). "The individual has to gain in the long-term for the organization to gain in the long-term" (Porras & Bradford, 2004). However, OD values must find a way to meld with organizational reality. Honoring humanity at the core of practice is constant, but it will be more useful in a holistic orientation to the organization. Wirtenberg et al. (2004) put it best:

> The need in organizations to manifest socially responsible values and create win-win business results has never been greater. OD is in an excellent position to seize the opportunity to build bridges, find common ground, and address organizational and cultural divides. (p. 479)

Although the field is eclectic, lacking a unified definition or focus, OD is grounded in humanistic, data-based, systems approaches to change. Citing these as three essential components of OD, Waclawski and Church (2002) emphasize OD's normative and humanistic values as a distinguishing feature and note that OD efforts should be aimed at promoting both individual and organizational benefits: "Although balancing issues of effectiveness and profitability are certainly important for economic success and survival, we would argue that an OD approach does not prioritize these concerns over the human perspective" (Waclawski & Church, 2002, p. 9). Burke (1992) also summarized OD values: OD is an applied field that seeks to make cultural change in organizations. The field has a humanistic value orientation that is rooted in the field's early sensitivity training projects. OD views people's feelings as an equally important source of data as facts and figures and thoughts and opinions. OD views conflict (interpersonal or intergroup) as something that must be surfaced and dealt with directly rather than ignored, avoided, or manipulated. OD also values a spirit of inquiry and democracy. OD is data-driven and uses both quantitative and qualitative data to make organization diagnoses and interventions. OD results are ideally achieved democratically in a manner that seeks collaboration and conflict resolution and ensures its participants are free from coercion and arbitrary exercises of authority.

OD's humanistic, democratic stance distinguishes it from other types of organizational functions. These values also create compatibility with adult education's commitment to social justice and the facilitation of individual and collective good through learning. OD's insistence on preserving human dignity in the workplace has sometimes made it a target as "touchy feely," however it was once observed that "the soft stuff is the hard stuff" when it comes to dealing with human dynamics in the workplace. Further, given the widespread cases of corporate corruption and misdoing, there is a clear need for ethical leadership and change that OD has the potential to offer. OD work happens in the grey space in an organization that often finds the OD consultant serving multiple stakeholders with competing goals and interests.

Adult educators and human resource development professionals are engaged in OD in a variety of contexts including business, nonprofit, government, healthcare, and education. This book attempts to describe how these applied fields of practice can strengthen one another when applied in the context of facilitating organization change and development. I maintain the HRD field has foregone an OD value system, instead favoring a human performance perspective that puts profit goals and management needs first. This book attempts to reconnect HRD with the values of OD and help adult educators see how the goals of OD fit with a commitment to social justice and activism.

A DEFINITION OF OD

There are many definitions of OD and no single accepted one. Early OD focused on "first order" change or moderate adjustments to the organization, people, and processes, based on the psychological premise that an emotionally healthy person increases her or his potential to contribute to the organization. These initial ideas were instrumental in beginning OD's life in the applied world. From this point, individual behavior change became the mantra of OD and practitioners depended heavily on the original work in psychology to push OD applications. According to Greiner and Cummings

(2004), ". . . little attention was given to other issues facing organizations or to new theoretical development" (p. 378). As a result, OD practitioners over-relied on technique to build their practice, using new tools to address issues rather than accurate diagnosis (Porras & Bradford, 2004). "In the worst case, less proficient OD practitioners were the kid with a hammer who saw everything as a nail" (Porras & Bradford, 2004, p. 396).

During the 1970s and 1980s, OD began to mature maintaining its focus on the workforce, but broadening its applications to address the needs of individuals in their organizational framework (Greiner & Cummings, 2004). OD specialists started to indulge in everything from labor relations to service excellence to organizational learning. This random swing from one thing to the next has expanded the net of techniques and the eclecticism of the field's definitions and practices. "There is no agreement about what OD is. The field lacks a central, agreed-upon theory of change—or even approach to change" (Bradford & Burke, 2004, p. 370). There is lack of recognition about what constitutes good OD and its effectiveness in producing real change (Porras & Bradford, 2004).

"Second order" or contemporary OD characterizing the field today seeks more comprehensive change and responds to a range of issues including: individualized career development, performance management, group and team dynamics, diversity and multiculturalism, total quality management (TQM), life-work balance, organizational learning, knowledge management, globalization, organizational transformation, organizational culture, learning organizations, organization restructuring, reengineering, visioning and future search, and large scale change. Cummings and Worley (2005) offer a widely accepted OD definition in their popular textbook: "Organization development is a system wide application and transfer of behavioral science knowledge to the planned development, improvement, and reinforcement of the strategies, structures, and processes that lead to organization effectiveness" (p. 1).

This book offers a more critical approach to theory and practice than typical HRD or OD texts, in an effort to reclaim OD's original humanistic, democratic value system and to better connect this work with the practices and values of adult education. Given this perspective, the term "OD" in this book uses this definition: **Orga-**

nization development (OD) is an intentional, systemic process of facilitating change to improve an organization's well-being.

Let's break down the definition. The statement **Organization development is an intentional, systemic process of facilitating change** recognizes the aim and scope of OD: it is a deliberate, humane process that is based on fostering knowledge and reflection on organization issues considering the whole organization system and seeking the growth and improvement of individuals, groups, and the organization. The next statement, **to improve an organization's well-being,** widens the scope and responsibility of OD practice and embraces a holistic organization health (Goldman Schuyler, 2004a) perspective. The need for organizations to focus more on well-being is articulated in Senge et al. (2008):

> As Ray Anderson, CEO of Interface, puts it (quoting former U.S. Senator Gaylord Nelson), businesses need to wake up to the simple fact that "the economy is the wholly owned subsidiary of nature, not the other way around." Similarly, there can be no healthy economy without a stable and vibrant social order—just ask businesspeople trying to do business in corrupt, lawless, or extremely poor societies. (p. 103)

Many OD books speak of "enhancing productivity and profitability" to the exclusion of organization health. This book refers to organization performance as "well-being" and considers outcomes that encompass far more than profits and performance in creating healthy and humane organizations. Goldman Schuyler (2004a) defines "healthy" organizations as characterized by "reciprocal nourishment" or a state where:

> Neither partner [such as worker and management] seeks to take advantage of the other: organizations are designed to enable the growth and development of their members or workers (in the broadest sense, including managers), and individuals do their best to enhance the organization's long-term viability. (p. 58)

Organization health or well-being assumes that the organization provides good jobs to people who can develop and grow with the organization while making a living wage. An organization well-being perspective holds organizations accountable for creating outcomes that matter for its workers and other stakeholders. Healthy organizations support cultures where people have influence and control over decisions that affect them. Healthy organizations enhance community life by sustainability, low environmental impact, compassionate work practices, and good citizenship. Some may criticize this definition as impractical and perhaps even being naïve since many management texts will dismiss any discussion that shifts the focus away from profits and productivity, yet early, prominent and influential OD scholars advocated for organization health (Argyris, 1964, 1973; Hackman & Oldham, 1980). Goldman Schuyler builds on the health model that an ideal state of physical, mental, and social health is not merely the absence of disease. Organization health prevents "disease" or organization dysfunction and promotes well-being. Bruhn (2001), as cited in Goldman Schuyler, defines the health of the organization as incorporating body, mind, and spirit. Body refers to the structure, organization design, power use, communication processes, and work distribution. Mind incorporates organization learning, conflict management, change implementation, and the incorporation of underlying beliefs, goals, policies, and procedures. Spirit is what gives the organization vibrancy and vitality, defined by Bruhn as the core or heart of the organization. Goldman Schuyler suggests that organization health can be measured through the behaviors and relationships of organization members. I advocate that a healthy organization also values and pursues productivity and profit, but simultaneously pursues much more. Finally, an organization well-being perspective also adopts an anti-performative and anti-oppression stance.

Southwest Airlines is a good example of a company that seeks well-being rather than just profits. It is a rare success in an industry that is plagued with escalating costs, mergers, bankruptcy declarations, labor unrest, aging equipment, and customer anger. Southwest is the only airline that has been consistently profitable during volatile times, earning $645 million in 2007 (Nocera, 2008). Southwest's beloved cofounder and CEO of 37 years, Herbert Kelleher, retired in 2008. He is the type of leader who gets standing ovations from shareholders and advertisements publicly thanking him from the pilots' union. When asked about the secret of Southwest's success his stock response has been "You have to treat your employees like customers . . . When you treat them right, then they will treat your outside customers right" (Nocera, 2008, p. 15). Southwest is a company that has never had layoffs, even though Kelleher acknowledges that:

> We could have made more money if we furloughed people. But we don't do that. And we honor them constantly. Our people know that if they are sick, we will take care of them. If there are occasions for grief or joy, we will be there for them. They know that we value them as people, not just cogs in a machine. (Nocera, 2008, p. 16)

The company also was very savvy and hedged their fuel at $51 a barrel, allowing them to weather the current escalating costs of fuel. Southwest has proven that attention to matters beyond the bottom line pays off in earnings and employee loyalty through the creation of a healthy organization.

Many OD definitions focus on improving "performance," and "performance improvement" is a popular HRD mantra. HRD's performance orientation ignores organization well-being and is too narrow to address OD practice in a complex environment with multiple stakeholders. OD that extends beyond performance and productivity goals calls for systems-based, humane, sustainable goals; and responsible implementation that enhances the wider community. This definition captures the critical action research framework and departs from contemporary definitions and models of OD. It attempts to shift the analysis to a more critical level to understand power relations that often determine OD's path and outcome. The Critical Action Research Model does not assume that all OD practice is inherently logical, rational, or good. It offers tangible steps for implementing a more critical OD.

THE HISTORY AND ROOTS OF OD

Adult educators often eschew OD and human resource development processes assuming they are wedded to human capital theory and loyal to management interests. Yet, the field of OD was developed out of an interest in creating humane, democratic workplaces and implementing lasting change—much the same value set that adult education was founded on during the same time period. Adult education has historically valued humane change in the world through education. Like adult education, OD principles are useful in a range of contexts beyond corporations for addressing organization change and improvement. This book offers an alternative framework of OD that foregrounds the stakeholders and critiques OD practice that is not mindful, responsible, and sustainable. This section will provide a brief overview of how the OD field and its interventions emerged.

If you have ever belonged to an organization, chances are you have experienced teambuilding, data collection and problem solving around issues, attitude surveys, a range of management styles, and attempts at changing the system or culture. All of these common organization practices represent the historical development of OD, beginning in the 1940s by Kurt Lewin. The history of organization development is rich, influenced by many practitioners and disciplines. A useful way of tracking OD's history is to examine the development of particular OD interventions mentioned above. The following sections will introduce important interventions that mark the historical development of the OD field including laboratory training, action research and survey feedback, participative management, quality of worklife, and strategic change. See Cummings and Worley (2005) or French and Bell (1999) for full historical summaries.

Laboratory Training and the Emergence of OD

The field of OD was born in the 1940s when Kurt Lewin developed laboratory training, also known as the "T-group." The "T" stands for training or "training group." T-groups are small, unstructured groups that involve people reacting to data about their own behavior and interactions in a group. The first T-group was accidental, convened in 1946 by Kurt Lewin and a client who met to debrief following a leadership training program. They decided to invite the participants to sit in on the facilitators' daily post-session debriefings, forming the first T-group. The opportunity to reflect on the experience of the session and question assumptions and behaviors of facilitators and participants proved cathartic and more powerful than the actual leadership training. T-groups resulted in the discovery that feedback about group process is a valuable learning experience that had potential to transfer to work relationships at the home site (Cummings & Worley, 2005). Lewin was a pioneer in group dynamics whose "field theory and . . . conceptualizing about group dynamics, change processes, and action research profoundly influenced the people associated with the various stems of OD" (French & Bell, 1999, p. 33).

T-groups were expanded into business and industry due to the effort of Douglass McGregor at Union Carbide, Herbert Shepard and Robert Blake at Esso Standard Oil (now Exxon), and Douglas McGregor and Richard Beckhard at General Mills. Applications of T-group methods at these companies spawned the term "organization" development and led corporate personnel and industrial relations specialists to expand their roles to offer internal consulting services to managers through activities such as team building (Cummings & Worley, 1993). Beckhard (1997) suggests that team building (consisting of interpersonal competence, communications, and problem solving skills) became OD. It is of interest to note that the widespread use of flip-chart paper as a convenient method for recording, retrieving, and presenting data in OD activities was invented by Ronald Lippitt and Lee Bradford during the 1946 T-group sessions (French & Bell, 1999).

T-groups proved difficult to sustain since transferring learning from the group to the workplace was challenging. T-groups led to training of intact teams from the same organizations and helped shift the focus more to the organization level of analysis and the development of team building. Robert Tannenbaum is considered to have conducted some of the earliest "team building" sessions in 1952 and 1953 developing a process that brought managers together to address personal and organizational topics. Chris Argyris was one of the first to conduct team building with CEOs and top executives and later made significant contributions to the theory and research on laboratory training, OD, and organizational learning (French & Bell, 1999). Herbert Shepard's work in employee relations at Esso Standard Oil (now Exxon) and in community development activities also had a major impact on OD. He was one of the founders of the first doctoral program in OD at Case Institute of Technology in 1960.

Action Research and Survey Feedback

Action research was developed in the 1940s by Kurt Lewin, John Collier, and William Whyte based on their discovery that research had to be closely linked to action if organizations were to use it effectively to manage change. Action research is an iterative, collaborative effort between organization members and OD professionals (consultants or researchers). The steps of action research include collecting data about organizational problems or functioning; analyzing data to understand the issue; devising and implementing solutions to the issue or problem; and collecting additional data to assess the results. The process is iterative; that is, the cycles of data collection and action are often repeated and they inform future action. A key feature of action research is the systematic collection of survey data that is fed back to the client organization. Lewin intended the action research to be critical, yet in practice this aspect has been diluted. This book offers a critical action research model to reinvigorate the critique necessary for organizations to address the systemic problems that prevent them from making changes and solving problems. The Critical Action Research Model will be described in Chapter 2.

Rensis Likert, a contemporary of Lewin, is known as a pioneer who developed scientific approaches to attitude surveys and is best known for devising the widely used, five point Likert Scale. In an action research project, Likert and Floyd Mann administered a company-wide survey at Detroit Edison in 1948 to assess management and employee attitudes. They also created a unique feedback mechanism known as an "interlocking chain of conferences" where the major findings were cascaded from top management on down through the organization. Feedback was conducted in task groups with supervisors and their immediate subordinates discussing the data jointly. Survey feedback is widely used in all types of organizations today, particularly by organizations seeking to monitor their environment and progress toward building the type of culture the organization is seeking.

Participative Management

Participative management grew out of early OD practice and application of T-groups in an attempt to apply OD's humane and democratic principles to management. Participative management departs from traditional autocratic management styles that historically invited little participation or input from workers in running the organization. Traditional management models have advocated top-down management and communication, allowed little lateral interaction or teamwork, and controlled decision making from the top. Participative managers contrast traditional, authoritarian managers by engaging all levels of employees in decision making and problem solving. Contemporary forms of participative management include total quality management; quality circles; self-directed work teams; lateral, vertical, and diagonal communication initiatives; and large-scale, inclusive strategic planning. Participative management techniques have been found to increase productivity, quality, and satisfaction of workers across the organization. OD consultants are trained to help managers become more participative in their managerial practice. If you implement a participative management initiative, you should exercise some caution as some initiatives have been shown to be oppressive toward employees serving primarily to increase productivity and loyalty rather than give employees true input into the management of the organization (Gee, Hull & Lankshear, 1996).

Quality of Work Life and Sociotechnical Systems

The quality of work life (QWL) movement initially emphasized developing sociotechnical systems that enhanced worklife in organizations in the 1950s and 1960s and generally incorporated union-management cooperation, employee involvement, and self-directed work teams. The 1970s inflation and escalating energy costs caused the quality movement to shift toward being more competitive internationally and expand its focus to include additional workplace variables that affect employee productivity and satisfaction including reward systems, work flows, management styles, and the physical work environment. Typical QWL activities include: quality circles, employee involvement, and employee empowerment (Cummings & Worley, 1993).

Planned and Strategic Change

You have probably been affected by or implemented change. OD efforts generally stem from decisions to make a change that will result in a higher performing organization. Strategic change involves improving the alignment among an organization's environment, strategy, and organization design. Strategic change interventions include efforts to improve both the organization's relationship to its environment, and the fit between its technical, political, and, cultural systems. The need for strategic change is usually triggered by a major disruption to the organization such as the lifting of regulatory requirements, a technological breakthrough, or a new CEO from outside.

Strategic change draws heavily on open systems planning (Beckhard, 1969). This application assumes that an organization's environment and strategy can be described and analyzed and that gaps between environmental demands and organization responses can be reduced and performance improved. For instance, companies that anticipated the green movement did a good job of making strategic changes to position themselves well in the market. Today there is a strong demand for green construction materials, recycled materials, and efficient appliances and vehicles. Since Beckhard's introduction of open systems planning, organization change agents have used a range of large-scale or strategic change models involving multiple levels of the organization. Strategic change consultants usually possess the following competencies: competitive strategic planning, finance, marketing, team building, action research, and survey feedback. The strategic change phase has enhanced the relevance of OD in organizations.

The tools profiled in this section trace OD from its beginnings in the 1940s with the T-group to contemporary applications of participative management and integrated change efforts. OD is change-

and learning-oriented, and each of these tools helps make proactive changes in organization practices and policies. The next section discusses the change process in OD and profiles key change models used in OD.

OD: A PROCESS OF CHANGE

Organization development incorporates the processes of development and planned change. Cummings and Worley (2005) note that OD focuses on or results in a change to the organization system, fostering learning or knowledge transfer to the client system, and demonstrating evidence of or intention to improve the effectiveness of the client system.

Waclawski and Church (2002) define planned change as "A formal and planned response to targeted organization-wide issues, problems and challenges" (p. 9). Types of planned change include: technological innovation, training and development, new product development, managerial innovations, and organization reengineering. The values of planned change usually revolve around enhancing economic potential and creating a competitive advantage.

Organization development (OD) is planned change in an organizational context that focuses on building the organization's ability to assess its current functioning and achieve its future goals. OD is concerned with improving the overall system (the organization and its parts) in the larger context. OD is a field of social action and arena of scientific inquiry. Three components of OD are that it is a data-driven process using action research, a total systems approach to organizational change, and a normative and humanistic values-based approach that is conducted for the good of the individual, organization, and community (Waclawski & Church, 2002). OD's distinguishing feature is concern with the transfer of knowledge and skill such that the system is more able to manage change in the future. It is important to understand that all OD involves change management; however, change management may not involve OD.

OD is based on a social systems approach (Katz & Kahn, 1978). The systems approach views the organization as an inter-

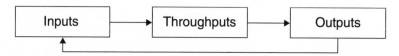

Figure 1.1 Diagram of a systems model

connected structure of interdependent subsystems such as: people, technology, processes, external environment, competitors, government, customers, and other stakeholders. Systems theory views the organization as drawing inputs from the outside world. Inputs might be raw materials, intellectual capital, human resources, new products or services, or technology.

A systems approach demands that the larger system be taken into account at all times. For instance, if customer satisfaction decreased, it is not enough to provide more training to the customer service representatives. The product, employees, management, work environment, response time, training, transportation and other variables must be considered to understand what other system factors might be affecting customer satisfaction. Figure 1.1 depicts a simple systems diagram. In this model, the organization is viewed as receiving input that is transformed into an output. All variables that affect both the input and throughput should be considered when conducting OD work (Cummings & Worley, 1993).

Inputs enter the system which transforms them into new products or services. These outputs are dispersed back into the environment and the process begins again. Another example would be the human body as a system. Simply put, the human body takes in oxygen. The input—oxygen—oxygenates the body and ensures survival. It is transformed into output or waste—carbon dioxide. This reoccurring system ensures our survival. The same systemic process happens within organization systems. For instance, in publishing, an input might be data (statistics, photos, techniques) that is transformed into useful information through analysis, organization, or synthesis (throughput) that is then delivered to the customer in the form of output (a report, book, or magazine). The systemic approach of OD is another distinguishing feature of the field. Other organizational approaches may take a piecemeal approach to addressing organization challenges. OD seeks to change the system.

OD is concerned not only with technical processes, but also human processes.

MODELS OF PLANNED CHANGE

Change is all around us and there is no shortage of consultants, books, and tools to help manage it. "Change is one of those words that serves as a melting pot for scores of concepts and methods. Like the Inuit expression for snow (of which there are 20 or more shades of meaning), change means many different things to us" (Ackerman, 1997, p. 45). To provide a common frame of reference for talking about change, Ackerman (1997) defines three types: developmental, transitional, and transformational. Developmental change involves growth and stretching to improve skills or methods at individual, group, or organization levels. Examples might include team building, problem solving, conflict resolution, meeting management, role negotiation, survey feedback, job enrichment, training, or market outreach (Ackerman, 1997). Transitional change strives to move toward a desired state over a specified period of time. Transitional changes might include reorganization, technology integration, new product development, mergers or acquisitions, and globalizing operations. Transitional change seeks to accommodate the new state and function effectively and is often viewed as a disruption to standard operating procedures. Transformational change results in a new state of being that was not known until it began to take form. There are many excellent resources on organizational change (Burke, 2008). Change is an important aspect of OD; however, if you seek to learn about change models and leading change, you should consult a resource focused on change specifically.

Cummings and Worley (2005) suggest that planned change models can be grouped into a four-step model of planned change:

1. Entering and contracting.
2. Diagnosing.
3. Planning and implementing change.
4. Evaluating and institutionalizing change.

Table 1.1 Comparisons of Planned Change Models

Lewin's Change Model	Action Research Model	Contemporary Action Research (Appreciative Inquiry)	Lippitt, Watson, and Westley's Phases of Planned Change	Critical Action Research Model
Unfreezing • Disconfirmation • Induction of guilt or anxiety • Creation of psychological safety	• Problem identification • Consultation with behavioral science expert • Data gathering and preliminary diagnosis	• Collect stories with broad participation	**Phase 1** • Development of a need for change **Phase 2** • Establishment of a change relationship	**Understanding** • Contracting and stakeholder identification • Defining reality: organization arrangements, power relations, stakeholders • Data collection, analysis, and diagnosis
Moving • Identification with new model • Scanning the environment	• Feedback to key client or group	• Examine data and develop possibility propositions	**Phase 3** • Working toward change • Diagnosis • Examination of alternatives • Actual change	**Critiquing** • Cultural analysis • Interests and values identification • Power relations • Interpretation and recommendations
Refreezing • Personal • Relations with others	• Joint diagnosis of the problem • Joint action planning	• Develop a vision with broad participation • Develop action plans	**Phase 4** • Generalization and stabilization of change **Phase 5** • Achieving a terminal relationship	**Learning** • Intervention • Implementation • Critical evaluation • Termination or recycle

Adapted from: Burke (1992); Cummings & Worley (2005).

You will notice these steps in some variation in the five planned change models featured in Table 1.1.

The planned change model has proven highly useful to the field of OD for over a half century. Planned change tends to be viewed as a rational, controlled, and orderly process, when in reality it is characterized by chaos, politics, shifting goals, discontinuous activities, unexpected events, and unintended outcomes. Planned change is also usually controlled by management, making it a managerialist approach to addressing organization challenges. Although planned change is common in organizations, the relation-ship between planned change and organization performance is poorly understood.

The execution of planned change also has several problems. OD practitioners tend to hone skills in particular areas that they may become partial to when recommending interventions and tend to overrely on these fixes such as: team building, total quality management, large-group interventions, gain sharing, diversity, re-engineering, organization learning and learning organizations, and self-managing work teams, to name a few. By using a "bag of tricks" to make planned change interventions, practitioners may overlook more appropriate interventions by reaching for what is convenient and easy when planning change. Other problems include that diag-nosis is done poorly due to time or money constraints, as well as faulty assumptions; management demands quick solutions or drives the change, excluding other stakeholders, and OD consultants oblige; and the organization does not respect the systemic nature of change.

Burke (1992) suggests that there are three models that pro-vide the underling framework for OD including the action research model, Lewin's three-step model of system change (unfreezing, moving, and refreezing), Schein's modified three-step model and phases of planned change according to Lippitt, Watson, and Westley (1958). Each will be discussed in the following sections, along with some other models of change.

Action Research

In 1946 Kurt Lewin was working in Connecticut with com-munity workers in the field of intergroup relations, but he found them "to be in a fog" because of a lack of clarity about what ought to be done. Lewin found this was due in large part to a lack of standards to measure progress, and advocated that without objec-tive standards of achievement, there can be no learning. He charac-terized the type of research needed as "comparative research on the conditions and effects of various forms of social action, and research leading to social action" (p. 202). And mere diagnosis (such as surveys) is not sufficient without research on the interven-tions.

He proposed a "spiral of steps each of which is composed of a circle of planning, action, and fact-finding about the result of the action" (p. 206). He called this action research.

Action research is a collaborative research method that actively engages participants in a systematic process that is critically oriented (not neutral), to develop, improve actions, and improve understandings and conditions. There is no one way to do action research. It has been called a mode of problem solving and it employs a variety of ways for systematic inquiry. Lewin's hope for cooperative action research as a way for human beings to solve their problems and manage their dilemmas illustrates how he fused democratic and scientific values (Bennis, Benne & Chin, 1961).

Contemporary forms of action research include: appreciative inquiry, participatory action, research, action learning, action science, and other action technologies (Brooks & Watkins, 1994). All forms can be viewed as extending action research toward more collaborative, systemic, and transformational processes. A comprehensive example of an action research project is captured in Rapoport, Bailyn, Fletcher, and Pruitt's 2002 book *Beyond Work-Family Balance: Advancing Gender Equity and Workplace Performance* where they worked with employees to collected data in an organization and were helped make substantive improvements to policies and culture around work-life balance issues. Other uses for action research might be to help workers deal with a reorganization by bringing the units together to examine the issues and challenges of creating new structures, or for teams to work on organization issues such as improving quality.

Lewin's Three-Step Model of System Change

One of the best-known models of change is Lewin's three-step model of system change (Figure 1.2). According to Lewin (1947), the nature of change is that it is an ongoing fluid process that has three stages known as unfreezing, moving, and refreezing. **Unfreezing** requires awareness of the need to change and desire to change it. Unfreezing may be facilitated through a problem or crisis, training, or data feedback from a survey. Unfreezing is challenging as Lewin noted it entails "unlocking the present social sys-

Figure 1.2 Lewin's model of change

tem" (Burke, 1992, p. 57) which may involve confrontation or re-education. An example of unfreezing is a nonprofit organization that adopted a fast growth strategy and began serving as many clients as possible, until it realized that maxing out services was going to prevent long-term growth and stability. The next step, **moving**, involves taking action that will change the system. It usually incorporates making interventions and providing other supports to actually implement the change. Movement interventions might include reorganizing, team building, or coaching. The nonprofit moved by revisiting its strategy and adjusting its service volume to preserve long term health. The third step, **refreezing**, is the process of reinforcing the change and making it permanent. Many changes fail when there is not infrastructure to support the movement that has occurred and conditions return to the pre-unfreezing state. Change, according to Lewin, is also characterized by forces that drive or restrain change from happening. Lewin's model is deceptively simple and easier said than done. The nonprofit's refreezing required revising its budget and goals, and adopting a longer-term focus for planning and goal setting.

Another contribution Lewin made to change theory was the development of the force field analysis (Figure 1.3) to depict opposing forces affecting the change. Both driving and restraining forces impact a change effort. The reason to conduct a force field analysis is to maximize forces driving the change, and minimize the forces restraining the change. For instance, in implementing self-directed work teams, driving forces might include interest among employees in having more control over their work. Restraining forces could be a management culture that is very top down that would cause employees to hesitate self-managing. Forces impacting reorganization are depicted in the example in Figure 1.3. Creating force field analyses can also be useful for individual and personal issues, such as changing habits related to health or wellness.

Forces Impacting Reorganization

Driving ➤	◄ Restraining
• Duplication of effort • Wasted resources • Poor communication • Outdated managerial or organizational structure	• Fear of change • Uncertainty • Anger • Resistance to change • Culture

Figure 1.3 Force field analysis example

Schein's Modifications on the Three-Step Model of Change

Schein (1987) elaborated on Lewin's three-step model by adding "how to's." Schein's model identifies three stages of unfreezing, moving or changing, and refreezing. He suggested that the stages occur rapidly and may overlap, but that it is important for OD consultants to identify which stage the system is in to provide effective guidance. At stage 1, Schein identifies three ways **unfreezing** happens including: (1) creating motivation and readiness to change through disconfirmation or lack of confirmation, (2) creating guilt or anxiety, and (3) providing psychological safety. Burke (1992) notes that employees will not embrace change unless they see a need for it. People see a need to change when their perceptions are disconfirmed such as an administrator receiving feedback that contradicts self-perception of a leadership ability. Lack of confirmation may simply be a belief that is not reinforced, such as being effective as a trainer. Both of these states may motivate a change. Creation of guilt or anxiety about a situation may propel change. Usually this state involves a gap analysis—or an understanding that the current state does not match the desired state. For instance, individuals who eat a poor diet or smoke may begin to feel guilty about their health in that it does not match their health goals or self-image. Anxiety over the anticipated health consequences may motivate change. Or a manager may feel guilty for being autocratic and embark on a change. Or faculty in a department at a university may realize that they are not meeting student needs or demand unless they begin to offer online classes. Neither disconfirmation nor induction of guilt is enough to motivate change, according to Schein. The last state, the creation of psychological safety, is key to unfreezing. People must believe that taking the next step will not cause them humiliation or loss of self-esteem. Consultants help with this stage by helping people experiencing change save face and feel safe. This means helping individuals make health changes by finding an exercise program where they do not feel self-conscious, or pointing out the strength of the manager's skills while also helping the person see the need for change, or providing training and assistance to faculty who feel inept at using new technology in front of much younger, more technologically proficient students.

Stage 2, **moving** or changing, incorporates two processes: (1) identifying with new role models and (2) environmental scanning. Once clients identify with a new role model, boss, mentor, or consultant, they can develop an appreciation for new viewpoints and even consider them for themselves. The consultant's job here is to help clients surface their own views or mental models and learn to appreciate those of others. This might involve helping the newly health conscious person reflect on how a healthier lifestyle leads to feeling better, asking the manager to envision developing a stronger team with new management skills, or for the faculty to become technological leaders on campus and generate revenue for their program. Environmental scanning can also be very helpful in moving clients toward change. This process helps the client learn what other organizations or leaders are doing and may provide valuable information to support the change.

The last stage, **refreezing**, is the process of helping the client to integrate the changes with the self and with others. Personal refreezing incorporates new ways of doing and thinking into one's self-concept. This means that new health habits are incorporated, new managerial leadership skills are applied, and new technology skills are used in teaching. The entire change process shares similarities with transformative learning which is heavily reliant on learning and reflection. It may take time and practice to implement a change and involve trying out new roles and behaviors, soliciting feedback, and making adjustments until the change is comfortable

(Burke, 1992). Relational refreezing is the process of helping the clients' new behaviors fit with significant others. For instance, when making health changes, it makes sense to involve family members, or when making management changes to involve colleagues and subordinates in understanding and supporting the change.

Lippitt, Watson, and Westley's Model of Planned Change

This model of planned change expands Lewin's three steps to five steps and changes the terminology from step to phases. Lippitt et al. (1958) assumed the perspective of the change agent in developing this model that could be internal or external to the organization and involved in the change process. The phases are:

1. Development of a need for change (Lewin's unfreezing).
2. Establishment of a change relationship.
3. Working toward change (moving).
4. Generalization and stabilization of change (refreezing).
5. Achieving a terminal relationship.

Lippitt et al. view phase 1, **development of a need for change**, happening in one of three ways: (1) a change agent creates awareness of a problem or need for change; (2) a third party sees a need for change and brings it to the change agent; or (3) the client system becomes aware of its needs and seeks the help of a consultant. Phase 2, **establishment of a change relationship**, suggests the creating of a collaborative partnership between the change agent and the client system. This is where you would come in as a consultant. In phase 3, **working toward change,** they suggest three subphases to include: (1) clarification or diagnosis of the client's problem via data collection and analysis; (2) examination of alternatives for addressing the issue; and (3) transformation of intentions into actual change efforts—implementation. The fourth phase, **refreezing**, involves spreading the change to other parts of the total system and creating infrastructure to support the change. This phase is most effective when affected parties are involved in the planning and implementation of the change. In the fifth phase, **termination**, Lippitt et al. advocate for ending the relationship between the client and consultant once the client has become independent of the consultant in maintaining the change. The client system becomes capable of problem solving and taking measures to maintain the changes and re-freezing.

Burke (1992) proposes a generic model for organizational change drawing on action research, Lewin's three steps, Schein's elaboration, and Lippitt et al.'s five phases of planned change. It includes:

1. An outside consultant or change agent.
2. The gathering of information (data) from the client system by the consultant for purposes of understanding more about the inherent nature of the system, determining major domains in need of change (problems), and reporting this information back to the client system so that appropriate action can be taken.
3. Collaborative planning between the consultant and the client system for purposes of change (action).
4. Implementation of the planned change, which is based on valid information (data) and is conducted by the client system, with the continuing help of the consultant.
5. Institutionalization of the change (pp. 62-63).

OD is concerned with helping organizations plan, respond to, and navigate change. Most change is accompanied by learning, so in addition to understanding change dynamics, it is of added import to understand adult learning and ensure that the change process is learner-friendly. Most change models incorporate Lewin's original steps of unfreezing, moving, and refreezing as strategies for moving through an effective change process.

CRITIQUES OF OD

OD has been a relevant field for over 60 years. The diversity and eclecticism of the field have caused some to criticize it and query whether it has lost its way. Despite practitioner loyalty to the profession, the field struggles to define OD's function and mission in the face of massive global change marked by ". . . a boundaryless economy, worldwide labor markets, instantly linked . . . communication, and agile new companies" (Lawler, n.d.). Many claim that as the world races by, organization development continues to be dismissed as faddish, as practitioners search for and offer the newest technique of the month to address a wide array of organizational issues (Bunker, Alban, & Lewicki, 2004; Porras & Bradford, 2004) without critically assessing their value or beneficiaries (Bierema & Fenwick, 2005). In the race to find the next OD fad fundamental questions such as "Whom does OD serve?" and "What is its mission in serving?" get lost in the shuffle. These are questions a critical OD poses.

Perhaps because of this lack of clarity about what constitutes good and effective OD, corporations do not always see OD interventions as an external solution to core decision making processes, like strategic development and mergers and acquisitions (Greiner & Cummings, 2004). OD has attempted to answer the call for managing change in the face of diversity, new technologies, and the economy. However, organizations don't want to just manage change, they "want to know how to produce it, control its pace, and cope with the effects" (Bunker, Alban, & Lewicki, 2004, p. 404). Organizations are looking now to meeting the needs of their external environment, while OD values are ". . . still concerned with empowering people so organizations could become more effective" (Greiner & Cummings, 2004, p. 382). This misalignment with the organization and its current global environment seems to give OD its lackluster appeal. OD is stuck in a groove, missing opportunities to play a larger organizational role, and suffering from a disjointed viewpoint.

Greiner and Cummings (2004) feel the OD field has a chance to reverse its obscurity by renewing its role as a vessel for change to "reach out and create integrative solutions for major strategic issues facing tomorrow's organizations" (p. 388). Wirtenberg, Abrams, and Ott (2004) suggest that OD specialists adequately prepare themselves to take on business challenges such as globalization, corporate social responsibility, workplace performance, technology integration, and evolving organizational partnerships. These are the emergent issues for which business leaders are seeking answers, and ones they are expecting OD specialists to transform into results.

A critical perspective provides the analytical tools to evaluate these rising issues.

Although OD's purpose continues to be debated in the field, it is a thriving and common practice in most organizations today. Seemingly, as long as there is desired change, there will be a place in the world for its facilitators: OD consultants. The critiques raised in this section also suggest that the OD field is ripe for a more critical approach, as outlined by this book.

SUMMARY

This chapter traced the development of the OD field and its interventions. The field emerged in the 1940s with the creation of laboratory training or T-groups. Lewin was a key figure in the development of many OD interventions, including the T-groups and action research. This work instigated the systematic study of work groups and practices aimed at improving their functioning. About the same time, action research surfaced as an iterative problem-solving process that involved data collection, analysis, intervention design, intervention, and evaluation. Survey feedback emerged after Lewin's death and continues to be used widely in organizations that are attempting to share feedback across hierarchical levels. Participative management developed to distinguish different types of management ranging from highly authoritative to participative. OD also was influenced by efforts to improve quality of worklife in organizations that focused on employee involvement in problem solving and decision making. OD aims to be strategic in planning and sustaining change and uses a systems model to conduct holistic analysis of problems and potential interventions. OD usually seeks to create some type of change and several change models have been proposed to describe this process. Lewin was again highly influential in the development of his three-step model of change that includes stages of unfreezing, moving, and refreezing. This model has been adapted by Schein and Lippitt, Watson, and Westley. Organization development and change are highly dependent on learning, making an understanding of the learning process so useful for consultants and others concerned with fostering change in organizations.

CHAPTER 2

Critical Perspectives

This book offers an alternative framework for organizational development that is influenced by critical management studies, feminist theory, critical HRD, critical cultural analysis, and a critical-interpretive approach. This chapter provides theoretical grounding in a critical OD practice in an effort to foster more socially responsible, mindful, democratic practice. This book assumes a critical perspective and defines OD as **an intentional, systemic process of facilitating change to improve an organization's well-being.** A critical OD practice challenges the status quo and replaces it with more democratic and equitable practices, policies, and structures. Critical management studies (CMS) provides a framework for addressing organization issues more critically in terms of who is privileged by organization practices and policies, and helps us understand how dominant power has become so enmeshed in organization life that we may not even notice the ways. CMS will be briefly discussed to help situate critical OD.

The phrase "critical management studies" first appeared in 1992 (Grey & Willmott, 2005, citing Alvesson & Willmott, 1992). Since that time, a number of factors have contributed to the rise of CMS including:

> The rise of managerialism associated with the hegemony of the New Right . . . the crisis of western (and especially North American) management in the face of global capitalism. . . . [and] the crisis of positivism in management research and the development of epistemological and methodological alternatives. (Grey & Willmott, 2005, p. 3)

Critical management studies seeks to foster insight, provide critique, and create a "transformative redefinition" of organization practices, cultures, and structures (Alvesson & Deetz, 2000). Wilmot (1997) describes CMS as "to envision and advance the development of discourses and practices that can facilitate the development of 'management' from a divisive technology of control into a collective means of emancipation" (p. 175). CMS questions prevailing management beliefs and practices and seeks to change them with the goal of disrupting the status quo and shifting power relations.

The management field has led the development of the CMS perspective with the goal of interrogating dominant, taken-for-granted assumptions of management. For instance, management thought and action tend to be viewed as objective, neutral, and scientific. "Managerialism" permeates the modern organization. That is, management receives the benefit of the doubt, is given prestige, and is assumed to have unquestioned authority. It is probably difficult to think of a manager who appreciates having management decisions questioned, yet this is what CMS aspires to do. CMS strives to emancipate workers and create more accountability for managers whose acts impact the lives of employees and other stakeholders (Alvesson & Willmott, 1996). Critical management thinking helps managers be responsible organization citizens and achieve socially and personally rewarding lives and careers (Porter, Muller, & Rehder, 1989). Perhaps the current financial crisis that was created by unchecked managerial decisions in making bad loans would not have happened if management actions were being questioned and critiqued.

Critical theory is a political theory that seeks to relentlessly criticize all existing conditions, especially those presumed "normal" like management or OD practices. Critical theory recognizes that structures of oppression and privilege characterize our lives and are often based on positionalities such as race, gender, sexual orientation, physical capability, age, class, or other visible and invisible markers. Critical theorists are interested in hegemony, or the way that people learn to accept unjust social systems as the natural state of affairs and in their own best interest. For instance, women in the organization may criticize the woman in the corner office, not realizing that their critiques make it harder for themselves and other women to ascend to leadership roles. "Hegemony" is also the process of dominant groups passing off the status quo as "normal" even though it oppresses the non-dominant groups. An example of this would be management explaining the lack of women executives by arguing that there are not enough women in the pipeline to have a pool of qualified candidates, even when women make up over 50% of managerial and administrative workers in the United States (US DOL, 2006). Another example of hegemony would be management expecting that non-managerial workers not question or challenge management's behaviors. This expectation will eventually result in workers not challenging management even when its behavior is blatantly inequitable or unethical.

CMS has been heavily influenced by critical theory and postmodernism and my perspective has also been informed by poststructural feminism that examines how interlocking positionalities shape human relations within shifting social contexts. These perspectives are committed to critiquing dominant ideology and discourse and acknowledging that human actors have fragmented identities (rather than being autonomous, self-determining individuals with a unitary identity) and positionalities. Critical theory and poststructural feminism critique metanarratives, or prevailing belief systems (Alvesson & Deetz, 2005), that dominate organization and even national thinking and discourse such as "change is a constant" or "change is a universally good process," or that "growth is desirable under all circumstances," or that "men should occupy the most prestigious positions in organizations." Alvesson and Willmott (1996) identified metaphors of organizations using critical theory to interrogate technocracy, mystification, cultural doping, and colonizing power of organizations. Alvesson and Deetz (2005) suggest that these metaphors:

> Draw attention to how management expertise leads to passivity on the part of other organizational participants, how ambiguity and contradictions are masked, how the engineering of values and definitions of reality tend to weaken lower-level and other marginal groups in the negotiation of workplace reality and respectively, how the codes of money and formal power exercise a close to hegemonic position over workplace experiences and articulated values and priorities . . . Critical

theory draws attention, for example to the narrow thinking associated with the domination of instrumental reason and the money code. (p. 81)

Examples of such dominant narrow thinking are evident in constrained work conditions where intrinsic work qualities such as creativity or meaningfulness are ignored or subordinated to instrumental values of productivity and profit; in the development and reinforcement of asymmetrical power relations, particularly between management elites and non-experts or workers; in gender bias; in extensive control of employees mindsets and a freezing of their social reality; in far-reaching control over employees, consumers, and the general political-ethical agenda in society through mass-media, lobbying, advocacy of consumerism and privileging of the money code as the measurement stick for success; and in the destruction of the natural environment through waste and pollution (Alvesson & Willmott, 2005). A critical approach involves pointing out silences and omissions. Clegg and Dunkerley (2005) lament,

> Our "issues"—sexism, power, capitalist development, organizational transactions and interactions, the historical interpenetration of state and capital—are not yet found in the indexes of most texts on organizations. We hope to remedy this state of affairs through posting this absence as problematic. Thus, it would seem no accident that the majority of texts on organization theory place greater emphasis upon concepts such as individual motivation, needs and satisfactions, than upon the structural features of power, exploitation, and historical change. (p. 47)

A critical stance challenges deeply held truths and shows how they serve to retain power among the powerful while oppressing the less powerful. For example, most people's image of a commanding executive is a white male. Even women and people of color may hold this image, making it more difficult when individuals in those roles do not fit the typical stereotype. Women in the corner office find not only their leadership scrutinized (as will most white males), but also their hair style, wardrobe, affect, and assertiveness. Nowhere has this double standard been more apparent than in the 2008 U.S. presidential election.

PRACTICAL REASONS FOR A CRITICAL OD

We can make several arguments for the value of a more critical approach to management, and hence OD. One is to prevent future exploitation of employees and stockholders by poor and unethical management practices. Another reason is to improve employee satisfaction and motivation. A 2000 Ethics Resource Center survey found that 43% of respondents believed their supervisors did not set good examples of integrity and felt pressured to compromise their organization's ethics on the job (Heesun, 2002). Monster Worldwide, a major internet job site in 23 countries, reported that 80% of those surveyed wanted a job with a positive environmental impact, and 92% preferred to work for an environmentally friendly organization (Senge, Smith, Kruschwitz, Laur, & Schley, 2008).

Not only do people want to work for an ethical employer, but also it is good business. Preston (2008) reports on a study that provides statistical evidence of socially responsible investing. The research was conducted by Bloomberg with the Genocide Intervention Network. Actual and forecast returns on investments of 37 multinational companies with interests in Sudan were examined. Sudan is a resource-rich country that has been accused of underwriting a genocide campaign against its Darfur citizens. It is estimated that over 450,000 have been killed and 2.5 million displaced. Annualized historical return on investment in 3 and 5 years and forecast returns for 2008 and 2009 were examined as study benchmarks. The research found that "Companies with links to regimes with questionable human rights practices make poor investments, financially as well as ethically" (Preston, 2008, p. 19). The highest human rights violators in the study underperformed peers by an average of 46% in year one, 22% in year three, and 7% in year five. They also underperformed for forecast returns on equity by an average of 6%. "The study findings are likely to give weight to shareholder proposals from divestment from companies linked to troubled regimes" (Preston, 2008, p. 19). Preston also notes that Fidelity Investments' shareholders voted to implement procedures for genocide investing and that other investment organizations are considering similar moves.

Dean's Beans, a coffee roaster, provides another good example of how social responsibility affects the organization's bottom line. The founder, Dean Cycon, says "our job is providing great coffee and helping coffee growers with whom we work around the world to thrive" (Senge et al., 2008, p. 327). In addition to improving the bottom line, a critical approach should improve decision making since it demands a more critically reflective process of examining options and making choices and giving voice to multiple interests. Critical approaches also provide a framework for raising tough questions, considering stakeholders, and committing to social responsibility. Organizations are under increasing scrutiny and pressure to be sustainable, global citizens. A critical framework helps move them in that direction. Finally, ethical and socially conscious organizations have been found to be more profitable and competitive (Preston, 2008; Verschoor, 1998).

FROM CRITICAL MANAGEMENT STUDIES
TO CRITICAL OD

HRD and OD have assimilated many taken-for-granted assumptions that privilege management and managers. This coopting of the fields into the hegemonic practices of management puts them at risk of being unable to fulfill their pivotal role of humanistically facilitating development and change. Change agents and consultants are required to meet the cliché of "thinking outside the box," challenging the status quo, and innovating in ways that help us see problems and opportunities in new lights. Yet, HRD and OD are increasingly thinking "inside the box" of capitalism and masculine rationality making it ever more difficult for the profession to behave ethically, sustainably, or creatively. Masculinist rationality is an assumption that masculine traits of objectivity, aggressiveness, and performance are the standard and that adhering to them is neutral behavior that should not be questioned. Usually these traits go unquestioned in organizations, and when they are challenged, the challenger is usually viewed as irrational, reactionary, and plain wrong.

The HR field in general is an excellent candidate for critical analysis as it has been historically applauded as a welcome movement away from Taylorist scientific management, and toward a more human and humane workplace. Yet, I maintain that the field is at risk of perpetuating the very philosophy it rose to challenge. Although many HR and OD innovations have been heralded as moving the workplace away from the external controls that have accompanied the rise of scientific management, today's innovations have been critiqued for simply moving the locus of control more toward the internal and self regulation, guided by what feminists call the panoptic gaze of the "other" as legitimate masculine authority. For instance, although workers today are valued for their whole person and treated humanely in the workplace, management has created means of worker surveillance such as monitoring communications that might be viewed as a kinder, gentler means of managerial control. These measures are subtle means of maintaining white male power, a vestige of management.

STRATEGIES FOR CRITICAL CHALLENGING

The previous section described CMS as a framework for practicing critical OD. This section features critical strategies for challenging current organizational arrangements and contesting practices. Strategies for challenging the status quo include: reflexivity, de-naturalization, and anti-performativity (Grey & Willmott, 2005).

Reflexivity

Reflexivity, a highly prized practice in both adult education and HRD, is a key critical competency. Adult educators may be more familiar with terms such as critical thinking, critical reflection, or reflective practice, and HRD practitioners may be more accustomed to fostering reflection through action learning or action science. Reflexivity involves a critical assessment of assumptions that frame thought and action. Both HRD and adult education have proven practices for helping learners consider and challenge assumptions. The critical perspective provides a platform from which we can challenge prevailing management and OD beliefs and practices. You can take a more critical approach to OD by reflecting on actions and questioning assumptions, particularly those that are taken for granted, and privilege certain groups over others.

De-naturalization

De-naturalization is crucial to oppositional politics and means that the prevailing order of things becomes taken for granted or naturalized and may even be referred to as legitimate, natural, or necessary, much like managerialism was described in the previous section. The prevailing order of things becomes "the way things are," or "the way we do things around here." "Of *course* men dominate women, whites dominate blacks, capital dominates labour. Whether based on evolution or social function, the answer is the same: There Is No Alternative" (Grey & Willmott, 2005, p. 5). In much the same way, management is privileged since the natural order of things is that of course management has more knowledge, deserves more money, and has earned a hierarchal position superior to other non-managerial workers. CMS serves to question these arrangements and "de-naturalizes" them. OD is well positioned to question organization arrangements and influence structure.

Anti-performativity

Anti-performativity is a special category of de-naturalization (Grey & Willmott, 2005). It challenges the notion that social relations should be "naturally" framed for their instrumentality. In other words, performativity means that social relations are managed to maximize output in the interest of productivity and profit. In educational terms, training would only be offered if it served to enhance productivity and profit, not because it would enhance relationships or the general learning or well-being of workers. Performativity is assumed to take priority over all other factors as the natural state of things and CMS aims to challenge this notion. Performativity has had a major influence in HRD. Critical OD serves to challenge this notion that knowledge and learning in organizations must ultimately serve the interests of management and the almighty dollar. It is important to note that anti-performativity does not mean anti-performance.

"Performative" is used in a somewhat technical sense to identify forms of action in which there is a means-ends calculus
that pays little or no attention to the question of ends. In effect, ethical and political questions and issues are unacknowl-
edged or assumed to be resolved. It follows that issues of a
fundamentally ethical and political character—such as the distribution of life chances within and by corporations or the
absence of any meaningful democracy from working life—
are ignored or if not ignored then only marginally adjusted
through, for example "involvement" and "consultation." Efforts are then directed at the matter of how limitations and
"dysfunctions" within the established system can be amelio-
rated without significantly changing or disrupting the prevailing order of privilege and disadvantage. (Grey & Willmott,
2005, p. 6)

CMS aims to challenge these arrangements, again, de-naturalizing
them.

Overwhelmingly, HRD and OD have been dominated by a
performance-based philosophy. They have conformed to conven-
tional management philosophy by embracing the components of
performativity. This is evident in the quest for bottom-line enhancing, productivity boosting practices that are measured with narrow
definitions of "return on investment" that may fail to consider the
humans doing the work. Performative concepts permeate many HRD
definitions. For instance HRD has been defined as "a process for
developing and unleashing human expertise through organization
development and personnel training and development for the purpose of improving performance" (Swanson & Holton, 2001, p. 4).
Nadler (1970) indicated "HRD is a series of organized activities
conducted within a specified time and designed to produce behavioral change" (in Swanson & Holton, 2001, p. 4). Carnevale was an
advocate for linking learning to the bottom line to improve the
company's competitive advantage. Swanson and Holton (2001) suggest that the idea of "improvement" is inherent in almost all definitions of HRD and that it is a "problem-defining and problem-solving process . . . focused on problems for the purpose of improvement"
(p. 16). Yet, often a bias toward improvement assumes deficiency:
Deficiency in the worker, the manager, the organization, the sys-

tem. The deficiency stance is laden with masculine, rational notions of management superiority and is challenged in critical OD. Adult education has focused in the opposite direction of HRD, embracing a critical, emancipatory agenda. Merging these two perspectives for OD practice will result in practices that are emancipatory and performance-enhancing.

ENVISIONING A CRITICAL OD

The conditions of our lives (including institutions and values) often prevent the acquisition of competencies necessary to fulfill potential. Critical theorists view power as a commodity with different groups holding varying degrees of it. Critical OD consultants have a responsibility to be reflexive and question prevailing assumptions and arrangements in organizations, and use their role to create new, more equitable structures.

When a critical perspective is brought to OD, it means viewing management as a political, social practice that has been influenced by historical and cultural power relations. These dynamics serve to privilege some organization members while marginalizing others. A critical OD acknowledges that its practices are dominated by a masculine epistemology that has historically served to preserve power relations in a manner that marginalizes women, people of color, and non-managerial workers. This masculine epistemology may manifest in performative value systems that effectively devalue, ignore, and silence non-dominant groups, preserving patriarchal and capital power in both theory and practice. Critical OD seeks to encourage egalitarian practices and policies in organizations, and requires vigilance on behalf of the consultant to uphold critical values.

Critical OD requires that the traditional standards of performance measurement be challenged and more socially conscious performance measures be devised that are aligned with organization well-being principles. If performance improvement is the organization's ultimate goal, then learning serves not as an end to human growth, but rather as a means to corporate growth. The goal and rhetoric of performance improvement have become OD's dominant discourse. Striving for performance is an acceptable goal, but OD must continually question its assumptions and beneficiaries and consider just what constitutes "performance." OD needs to measure performance beyond profit and productivity to include broader issues such as ecological impact, cultural impact, economic impact, political impact, and global impact. A critical OD functions to elevate OD's gaze to the broader horizon in the creation and pursuit of its goals.

A critical OD would help organizations be more accountable to stakeholders by ensuring a living wage was provided to all workers, and that "success" was redefined to mean more than profitability to include organization health or well-being. OD could lead in the development of instruments to evaluate organizations based on their overall health, ethics, environment, economics, stakeholders, fairness, diversity, social responsibility, sustainability, and living wage, not simply money earned. OD also has the potential to help create employee managed and owned organizations that are accessible to all employees regardless of gender, race, class, religion, physical ability, or sexuality.

Perhaps the only reason OD professionals have not been indicted in the recent epidemic of corporate ethics atrocities is attributed only to the dominant obsession with the financial side of business. In an alternative world, OD would have been on the stand for failing to hire, train, promote, or monitor employees effectively. Critical approaches seek transformation that makes the world a more equitable place. A critical OD could help transform management from a rational, bureaucratic, hierarchical, masculine practice to one that is nonlinear, flat, and more parallel to natural models (Helgesen, 1990; Wheatley, 1992).

It has been argued that a theory is only critical if it describes what is wrong with current social reality, identifies actors to change it, and provides clear norms for criticism and practical goals for the future (Bohman, 1996). A critical approach to organization change and development represents a shift in a new direction. I am not advocating against performance, but believe consultants have an obligation to be anti-performative with openness toward measuring outcomes more broadly. In other words, we want to see our organizations perform well because that ensures livelihood for both workers and the organization. But, performance enhancements with little other consideration of stakeholders or organization well-being are not desirable (performative). By skewing its focus toward managerial and monetary interests, both OD and HRD abandon their humanitarian roots. Putting critical principles into action will be further discussed in the book's framework that considers the consultant, the stakeholders, the context, and the interventions.

CRITICAL ACTION RESEARCH
AND CONSULTING PHASES

This section introduces the book's framework, the Critical Action Research Model, and phases of consulting.

Framework of the Book

The framework for this book considers OD from the four aspects of consultant, stakeholders, context, and interventions, while applying a Critical Action Research Model.

The OD Consultant

The OD consultant refers to the diverse range of individuals who practice OD. You may or may not think of yourself as an OD consultant. Adult educators and human resource practitioners often conduct OD in the context of their work as they strive to help individuals meet their goals and implement changes to improve organizations. OD consultants can be either internal or external to the organization and possess a range of competencies that have been defined as useful in OD. For instance, an OD practitioner may be an internal consultant who specializes in group dynamics and organization diagnosis. As you will see in Chapter 3, there are a wide range of competencies for the OD consultant and no one person will or should acquire them all. It is really up to you to decide what you want to specialize in as an OD consultant. OD consultants usually follow a consulting protocol and use an action research method.

The OD Stakeholders

Stakeholders in the OD process are many and will be further discussed in Chapter 4. They include not only employees and management, but also clients, customers, and the wider community, not to mention you as the OD consultant. Mindfulness of stakeholders means that you value social responsibility and sustainability in your work. As OD consultants, we are also in a unique position to educate organizations about their responsibility to stakeholders and influence the process for their benefit.

The OD Context

Social, political, and cultural factors put pressure on employees and organizations alike. Contemporary organizations operate in a complicated system (or context) that is significantly influenced by globalization resulting in new governments, markets, and economies, and an increasingly diverse workforce and customer base. The technology explosion also impacts workers and organizations in terms of the volume of information that must be managed and the development of e-commerce. Organizations are under constant pressure from shareholders to be "nimble and quick" in their structure, markets, and policies and are in a state of continual flux as the global context changes. Organizations and workers are plagued with restructuring and downsizing edicts, ethical indiscretion, and threats of moving overseas. In the midst of multiple and sometimes competing pressures, some stakeholders are privileged, while others experience hardship as organization life plays out. Often, management is advantaged when the organization is going through change. OD is valuable in this shifting context since it can help interpret the political climate and culture, and heighten awareness of and cater to stakeholders as organizations go about becoming more flexible, adaptive, and effective. Many organizational books take a *Fortune 500* perspective, targeting their examples and interventions toward corporate environs. This book will expand the context beyond the corporate sector to include nonprofit, education, government and other noncorporate entities, since the work of OD is critically important in these settings. Chapter 5 discusses contextual factors affecting OD.

The OD Interventions

The practice of OD is varied and rich. A wide range of models and tools exists to address planned change in organizations through processes such as action research, individual-based strategies including career development and mentoring, group and team-based strategies such as team building and conflict resolution, and organization and large-scale-based strategies such as reorganization or vision development. Chapter 6 will discuss interventions that are critical in nature to help you have more impact in facilitating change.

THE CRITICAL ACTION RESEARCH MODEL

In the Critical Action Research Framework, the OD consultant assumes an activist role with the objective of upholding the critical OD process. Action research strives to improve processes and practices while simultaneously learning about them, the organization, and the change process itself. Action research has been described as a process according to French and Bell (1999):

> Action research is the process of systematically collecting research data about an ongoing system relative to some objective, goal, or need of that system; feeding these data back into to the system; taking actions by altering selected variables within the system based both on the data and on hypotheses; and evaluating the results of actions by collecting more data. (p. 130)

They also define action research as a problem solving approach: "Action research is the application of the scientific method of fact-finding and experimentation to practical problems requiring action solutions and involving the collaboration and cooperation of scientists, practitioners, and laypersons" (p. 131).

The words *action research* reverse the actual sequence (Brown, 1972) in that "research is conducted first and then action is taken as a direct result of what the research data are interpreted to indicate" (Burke, 1992, p. 54). Action research is an iterative process that entails data collection, analysis, intervention, and evaluation. The process is a cycle that will lead to spiraling knowledge and that is useful for addressing the organization issue. Action research is powerful because it involves key stakeholders in the data collection and analysis, intervention, and evaluation. Although the process is usually guided by a consultant, it will only be effective if the problem owners are intimately involved in and accountable for the process. Action research is a process in two different ways. It is a sequence of events and activities *within each iteration* (data collection, feedback and taking action based on the data); and it is a *cycle of iterations* of these activities sometimes treating the same problem several times and then moving to different problems.

Although it is imperative for us as consultants to show self-restraint and let the client solve the problem, our role is also to influence the process. This book is focused on adult educators and human resource development professionals who are engaged in change work. The book also embraces adult education's commitment to social justice and adopts a critical HRD framework. Therefore, OD in this sense is focused on improving society and creating change and processes in organizations that are representative of stakeholder interests and responsible for creating sustainable, humane organizations. This model of action research attempts to insert a more political, cultural analysis than typical organization development models do. As was demonstrated in previous chapters, the prevailing OD and HRD texts do not adequately address power relations. I contend that OD is a political process that unchecked, may skew its interests toward management, performativity, and the creation or maintenance of inequitable workplaces.

I used a critical-interpretive approach (Alvesson, 1996; Deetz & Kersten, 1983) to reframe the traditional action research model into three major phases of understanding, critiquing, and learning. Understanding requires developing awareness that organization conditions are not composed of unchanging structures devoid of human influence, nor are they objective and rational. Instead, organization conditions are human creations that are mutable. In this model, *understanding* incorporates the action research steps of *contracting and defining organization realities through data collection, analysis, and diagnosis* in a way that helps us understand the context.

The second step of a critical-interpretive approach involves critique. *Critique* recognizes that organizations are socially constructed and value-laden reflecting asymmetrical power relations and competing interests. Critique in this model will involve *conducting an analysis of culture and power relations and providing feedback*

1. Understanding the Context
  a. Contracting and stakeholder identification
  b. Defining reality: Organization arrangements, power relations, stakeholders
  c. Data collection, analysis, and diagnosis
2. Critiquing Influences on the Issue
  a. Analysis of culture and power relations
  b. Feedback to the client
3. Learning through Action and Reflection
  a. Intervention implementation
  b. Reflection on the learning process
  c. Termination or recycle

Figure 2.1 The Critical Action Research Model

to the client. It depends on applying the strategies of reflexivity and denaturalization as described in Chapter 1.

The third step of the approach is the *learning* phase. It is concerned with creating meaningful change by building upon understanding and critique. In this model, learning incorporates *interpretation of the understanding and critique steps, determining and implementing action, and critical evaluation of the results.* This is similar to an action learning approach with iterative cycles of action and reflection. A diagram of the model is in Figure 2.1. This model will help adult educators and HRD practitioners engage in more critical and reflective OD.

Phase 1: Understanding the Context

The first major step of the Critical Action Research Model is to build understanding about the client and the context. This involves three major steps: (a) contracting and stakeholder identification; (b) defining reality (organization arrangements, power relations, stakeholders); and (c) data collection, analysis, and diagnosis.

a. Contracting and Stakeholder Identification

As consultants, we gain entry to organizations in a variety of ways. The client may contact us, or vice versa. A third party may recommend that the client contact us and so we initiate a relationship. Regardless of how entry is accomplished, it is important to remember that consulting is a process of building effective relationships based on trust and openness. If you cannot put your clients at ease, it is unlikely that they will be open about the problem or satisfied with your work. Clients may be initially suspicious or resentful of your presence, especially if they feel a consultant has been imposed on them or the organization. The initial meetings can be stressful for both you and the clients. It is important to maintain a positive self-image and make sure you are grounded before meeting with the clients. In addition to being self-confident, you need to be open with your clients about your opinions and feelings, what Block (1999) calls authenticity. If you are dishonest, exaggerate your skills, or try to manipulate clients, you can expect problems related to trust and satisfaction with your work.

When contracting, it is of vital importance to articulate the mutual expectations of the relationship, identify who will do what, delineate any boundaries that may exist, and determine what data will be used and how it will be handled. It also requires correct identification of the primary client (and it may not be the person who initiated the consulting relationship). Block (1999) suggests it is at this time that you take the following actions.

- Ask direct questions about who the client is and who the less visible parties to the contract are.
- Elicit the client's expectations of you.
- Clearly and simply state what you want from the client.
- Say no or postpone a project that in your judgment has less than a 50/50 chance of success.
- Probe directly for the client's underlying concerns about losing control.
- Probe directly for the client's underlying concerns about exposure and vulnerability.
- Give direct verbal support to the client.
- Hold frank discussions with the client when the contracting meeting is not going well.
- Devise a contract that ideally consists of the following:
  - Contact information.
  - A statement about the purpose, objectives, procedures, and

evaluation of the project.
- A timeline or Gantt chart.
- Identification of who will be involved and assignment of responsibilities.
- Identification and resolution of potentially difficult issues such as confidentiality, methodology, levels of involvement, and authorship (if there will be printed material based on the intervention).
- A statement acknowledging the dynamic nature of the contract and giving permission for either party to request renegotiation as necessary.
- A project management plan including separation and disengagement of the consultant.
- A budget (p 58).

Once the contract is agreed upon, the consultant can focus the next steps to help understand the context.

b. Defining Reality

Defining reality requires you to be a savvy observer of the organization context including power relations and positionality. It also requires awareness of how clients might respond negatively or resist the consulting process. Clients may feel trepidation or distrust when they begin working with you. They may be on the defensive, which can make establishing trust and credibility challenging. There may be positionality issues if, for example, your gender, age, or race is not what the clients expected. The clients may be afraid that you will make them look bad. This may cause them to withhold information from you at first. Preserving individual and organizational integrity of the clients must be foremost in your mind. Clients may also expect to shift their problem to you or that you will solve their problem and implement the fix. Neither of these is desirable, making establishing expectations upfront paramount.

There are both formal and informal discussion points that need to be covered during the contracting phase. The formal issues consist of deciding what service or activity will be provided within a specific timeframe, and establishing a budget for how much the intervention will cost. For instance, if a client wants you to conduct a needs assessment, you need to decide when it will occur and how much money is available for both data collection and your services. You also need to have informal information on key relationships and interpersonal dynamics in the organization, what approaches will work best in the culture, the level of commitment expected by the client, whether there is a match between value systems, and how and when the consulting relationship will be terminated. It is imperative to get these arrangements agreed upon and written down, in the form of a consulting contract.

c. Data Collection, Analysis, and Diagnosis

It is important that you work collaboratively with the clients to determine how to collect data. OD almost always involves some type of research to build an understanding of the problem. For instance, a nonprofit organization might survey its donors or beneficiaries before engaging in strategic planning. Or a governmental department may conduct a needs analysis prior to a training program. Or, a corporation might conduct an attitude survey before embarking on a culture change initiative. The following are common data sources used in OD: interviews, questionnaires, direct observation, document analysis, experience and intuition, critical incidents, surveys, focus groups, personality assessments, team interventions, process observation and consultation, action learning, appreciative inquiry, future search conferences, and action research.

OD is a mutual endeavor between the clients and you, making it imperative that the data collection process is joint. Establishing a partnership with the clients in the data collection process usually strengthens their commitment to and investment in the eventual OD intervention. You can serve an important role during the data collection to help the clients distinguish between cause and effect, and investigate both the problem and its management. Usually your expertise with research is helpful to clients when planning the data collection phase. You can also help clients see the problem more broadly by understanding what factors contribute to the problem and how this fits within the larger context of the organization and its management.

When analyzing data, it is important to consider different levels of analysis and categories of problems. OD may be directed on the individual, group, organization or system level. Categories of problems may relate to structure, people, rewards, procedures, or technology. Structure involves understanding how reporting relationships are arranged and how formal and informal power relations affect the organization. People issues tend to focus on relationships, leadership, training, communication channels, how people feel, the level of motivation and morale, and understanding the organization culture. Rewards systems include financial and non-financial incentives available for performance and perceived equity among employees. Procedures such as decision making processes, formal communication channels, and policies and procedures also form an important category for analysis. Finally, technology involves assessing whether the organization has the necessary equipment, machinery, technology, information, and transport to accomplish its tasks.

Phase 2: Critiquing Influences on the Issue

The next phase of the Critical Action Research Model critiquing influences on the issue, involves (a) analysis of culture and power relations, and (b) feedback to the client. Throughout the process it is important to be mindful of how your presence is affecting the process and how interests and power are being negotiated.

a. Analysis of Culture and Power Relations

It is essential to accurately identify cultural forces and power relations when consulting. One way this can be accomplished is by anticipating the form that defensiveness or resistance might take since these behaviors offer clues to the organization's interpersonal dynamics. For instance, if you were assessing retention issues and had data that women and men of color were leaving due to discrimination and harassment, you might anticipate denial and defensiveness from the client. Planning to have benchmarking data on other organizations or information on the business case for diversity would be two ways of counteracting this defensiveness. In addition to defensiveness, clients are often resistant to making changes. It is important to anticipate what issues might arise in resisting making a change (it will cost too much, we don't have time, and so forth) and identify the questions you can ask related to these issues. Senge et al. (1994) offer excellent strategies for confronting resistance. It can also be a good idea to invite those you anticipate to be most resistant so that they become involved in determining the intervention. It also helps tamper their resistance if clients are involved in the intervention planning and implementation and have full information about the problem and intended intervention. You also need to identify people who will be missing from the meeting, but have a stake in the outcome and follow up with them as appropriate. Finally, you also need to plan strategies for soliciting feedback on the consultation during the meeting.

b. Feedback to the Client

Once the data are collected and analyzed, it is time to communicate them to the client. Usually this is accomplished through a feedback meeting. As a consultant, it is vital to be clear about what you want from the meeting. It might be a better understanding of the problem, agreement on a course of action, and/or further work with the client. Structure the meeting so that you have adequate time for both data analysis presentation and dialogue. When sharing feedback, it is critical to be non-evaluative and descriptive. It is also helpful to anticipate aspects of the feedback that are likely to cause client defensiveness and plan to defuse them.

Cummings and Worley (2005) suggest that feedback is most useful when it is relevant to the stakeholders, and presented in a way that is understandable and descriptive, verifiable, timely, limited (as in do not overload the client with more than can be processed at one time), significant, comparative, and unfinalized. In addition to providing well-packaged feedback to the client, it is imperative to provide constructive feedback to the client. This means sharing both what is going well and what needs to be improved. In all cases the feedback must be clear (what behaviors are resulting in success or failure?). Remember not to sugarcoat unfavorable feedback, and be careful that it does not come across lacking in specificity or as hurtful and insulting. It must be specific and backed up with the data collected.

As a consultant, you are responsible for taking certain steps to effectively manage the feedback meeting such as providing the client access to all the information collected. It is important to have established data use in the contracting process. If you are collecting sensitive data such as an attitude survey in an organization where employees are unhappy, you will want to take appropriate research measures to protect the confidentiality and anonymity of participants. You want to make sure this type of measure is agreed on in writing with the client. That gives you backup should the client ever demand access to raw data. Sharing it would be unethical. In one case where a company president demanded raw data from an attitude survey that was highly negative, the consultant wound up quitting and taking all the data, rather than violate personal ethics and turn the data over to the president, who claimed the company "owned" the data because the company had paid for the survey.

In addition to sharing data with the client, you will probably not use all of the data collected. It is your job to synthesize the data so that it is useful to the client and present what is needed to move forward on the issue. You will want to ensure that data are balanced and include success data in addition to the "failure" data. Again, it is imperative to respect confidentiality and anonymity. This stance will enhance your integrity. It is important to include data that calls attention to the root cause as well as the symptoms (often the presenting problem) and that it not be sugarcoated to make it more palatable to the client. The feedback meeting also should highlight data in areas where the client has responsibility and authority to make changes, and use data to highlight a manageable number of problems. It is also helpful to include data the client will view as important that calls attention to problems where there is a commitment to change. Do not inundate the client with detail. Do not allow the client to project frustration about the data onto you. Be prepared to deal with resistance, and invite the client's assessment of the problems and courses of action.

There are some key considerations to make when giving feedback to ensure that the process is effective. According to Block (1999), it is important to be assertive and use language that is descriptive, focused, specific, brief, and simple. It is recommended that you avoid language that is judgmental, global, stereotyped, lengthy, or complicated. The feedback presentation is generally structured around three points: (1) analysis of the technical or business problem; (2) analysis of how the problem is being managed; and (3) recommendations for intervention. Block (1999) offers a useful meeting agenda to follow for a feedback session:

1. Restate the original contract.
2. State the purpose, outcomes, and process for the meeting.
3. Present diagnosis.
4. Present recommendations.
5. Ask for client reactions.
6. Be authentic—ask the client during the meeting, "Are you getting what you want?" "Is this meeting your expectations?"
7. Make a decision on actions or next steps.
8. Address concerns and assess commitment.
9. Reflect on whether or not your goals were met.
10. Be supportive.

Block suggests structuring the presentation by making a statement of the problem, discussing why the problem exists, and considering what will happen if the problem is not fixed in both the short term and the long term. Next, recommended solutions should be generated and anticipated benefits identified. Once the feedback meeting is completed, it is a good idea to conduct a meeting post mortem. This involves evaluating the meeting and reflecting on what happened, soliciting input from stakeholders.

Phase 3: Learning through Action and Reflection

Now that you have completed the first two phases of the Critical Action Research Model, you are ready to move to Phase 3, learning through action and reflection. This phase involves (a) intervention implementation, (b) reflection on the learning process, and (c) termination or recycle.

a. Intervention Implementation

Now that data have been analyzed and shared with the client, and an intervention agreed upon, it is time to implement the solution. "Implementation is . . . the point of the consultation" (Block, 1999, p. 247). This step is essential to ensure client ownership, leadership, capability, and organization of the intervention. It is a mistake to allow the client to push ownership off on you as the consultant and measures need to be taken to make sure that the ownership of the change is held by the client. The degree to which ownership of change occurs depends on availability of information about the change, the level of the client's participation in decision making, the level of trust in the change champion, previous experiences with change, the degree of impact on relationships, and individual personalities. You also need to watch for signs of low client commitment which include anger, hostility, objections, unwillingness to look at the options, unwillingness to look at the process issues, hidden agendas, delaying tactics, and failure to implement. To successfully make an intervention, there must be commitment and leadership from the top, individual competence, and adequate organization.

As a consultant, you have a range of options during the implementation. You can elect to stay out of the way, take a "hands-on" approach, or serve as facilitator. Cockman et al. (1996) advocate the facilitative role as most desirable and offer these guidelines for helping facilitate implementation:

- Provide support and encouragement.
- Observe and share feedback.
- Listen and offer counsel when things go wrong.
- Help the client modify and fine tune the plan.
- Identify process problems that impede implementation.
- Bring together parts of the client system to address process issues (conflict, communication, etc.).
- Bring people together from different disciplines or different parts of the organization to work on implementation.
- Organize necessary training and education.
- Work with managers to help them support the change process.
- Confront inconsistencies between the plan and how it transpires.

Block (1999) cautions us to not view the implementation process as a rational one. It is a messy and challenging process for individuals and organizations to shift their thinking and change their behavior. Since implementation requires unlearning and re-learning, adult educators are at a particular advantage, because they understand the cognitive, affective, and behavioral aspects of learning in a way that can facilitate the design and oversight of the implementation. Once the intervention has been made, it is time to start evaluating the situation. At this point the OD phases may begin again following the steps of entry and contracting, data collection and diagnosis, feedback, and intervention. Eventually, the consulting relationship will terminate.

b. Reflection on the Learning Process

Reflexivity, the critical assessment of assumptions framing thought and action, is a core competency for critical challenging. Throughout the action research process, it is valuable to foster on-going reflection in and on action. You can facilitate such reflection among client stakeholders and it is helpful to also be actively engaged in reflection on your own performance as this is a key opportunity to improve your own practice. The action learning model is highly effective for providing a structured process for taking action, reflecting on outcomes, and taking future action.

c. Termination or Recycle

All consulting jobs end. Successful disengagement is indicative of an effective intervention and implementation. Here are the steps to disengagement:

1. Develop members of the client department to take over your role.
2. Agree during contracting to sequential reductions in your time frame and budget as the implementation progresses.
3. Plan a collaborative event that terminates the project such as a report, celebration, article, or publication.
4. Agree on a minimal support maintenance plan. This might be periodic meetings, observations, or reports.
5. Agree to an end point celebration to acknowledge achievements.

To ensure a smooth concluding point remember that disengagement and needed follow-up are important consulting responsibilities, and your job in this role is to become redundant and work yourself out of a job. This is how you get repeat business. All contracts should have a disengagement plan and it is best to disengage post-implementation. You need to guard against managers seeking to end the implementation prematurely, particularly when they are tasked to change. If things go badly or not as planned, ask for feedback. This can help preserve or build trust and help you learn.

It is a good idea to create the expectation that you will disengage from the consulting relationship during the implementation or even before. When you formally terminate, it is important to formally acknowledge the ending. This may be more difficult for internal consultants who will be looked to for follow-up and ongoing support.

Longer term projects may require a recycling of the critical action research process where the organization is continually building its capacity and problem solving abilities. The recycle would mean that the consultant takes the client through the process, perhaps improving on changes already implemented.

SUMMARY

This chapter introduced critical perspectives for OD by drawing on critical management studies—CMS. CMS has emerged as a theoretical framework to contest dominant management theory and discourse which values performativity and instrumentalist goals. A more critical stance aims to disrupt thought and practice by challenging taken-for-granted beliefs and actions, such as privileging management above other workers or the unbridled pursuit of growth and market dominance. CMS offers the strategies of reflexivity, denaturalization, and anti-performativity as tools for challenging current organizational arrangements. The second part of the chapter introduced the book's framework that features the consultant, stakeholders, context, and interventions. The chapter also introduced the Critical Action Research Model that reframes the traditional action research and consulting process into a stage of building understanding through contracting, data collection and analysis, and diagnosis. The next stage is critiquing the organization culture and power relationships and providing feedback to the client. The final stage is learning and incorporates interpreting the first two stages (understanding and critiquing), implementing action, and critically evaluating the results.

CHAPTER 3

The Critical Consultant

The framework for this book considers OD from the four perspectives of the consultant, stakeholders, context, and interventions, while applying the Critical Action Research Model. This chapter focuses on the OD consultant by identifying the different types of consultants, defining traditional OD competencies and skills, and distinguishing the critical OD consultant from a traditional consultant.

Your goal as a consultant, in addition to making an intervention, is to establish a collaborative relationship with the client, help solve problems permanently, and develop client commitment and ability to maintain the change once the consultancy ends. Consulting is a highly educative and developmental process, and one that adult educators and HRD professionals are perfectly equipped to facilitate. You may be called into an organization to create a new performance management system and in the process educate the client about diversity and research in ways that improve the organization's capacity to develop a diverse workforce and solve its own problems.

A consultant is a person in a position to have some influence over a group or an organization, who generally has no direct power to make changes or implement programs within the group or organization (Block, 1981). Although you may have been hired to conduct a cultural audit, convincing the organization to address cultural issues will be much more challenging than the act of data collection itself. It requires influence! Consultants are:

People who find themselves having to influence other people, or advise them about possible courses of action to improve the effectiveness of any aspect of their operations, without any formal authority over them or choosing not to use what authority they have. (Cockman, Evans & Reynolds, 1996, p. 3)

Consulting is a multifaceted and challenging work and there are many types of consultants.

TYPES OF OD CONSULTANTS

Framed artwork hanging in my office recommends, "Let's hire a consultant so we have someone to blame" (David Bigelow). Your savvy as an OD consultant will help you avoid contracting with clients who are looking for a scapegoat and it is important to not let clients make their problem your problem. It takes skill and practice to effectively establish relationships, roles, and responsibilities with clients that are mutually beneficial. OD consultants work in a variety of organizations and functions such as accounting and audit, computing and IT, corporate planning, industrial relations, occupational health, operational research, organization development, career development and coaching, nonprofit, personnel services, productivity services, quality control, research and development, health and safety, training and development, and vocational counseling. There are different types of consultants, but regardless of the type of OD consultant you are, there are particular key competencies that will improve your ability to engage in effective, mindful OD. These include intrapersonal skills, interpersonal skills, general consultation skills, and knowledge of OD theory and practice. General consulting skills assume that you are using a particular model of planned change such as action research or critical action research. In addition to using a planned change model, you will bring your theoretical and practical knowledge about OD to the consultancy. This knowledge includes understanding the OD field, models of planned change, traditional and contemporary approaches to OD, and appropriate OD interventions. Finally, this chapter also advocates that you become a critical consultant and build an OD practice that is focused on organization well-being, stakeholder advocacy, authenticity, and activism.

One way to define a consultant is by whether you are an *internal* or *external consultant*. Internal consultants are permanent members of the organization, while external consultants have a temporary relationship with the organization. Each type of consultant has both advantages and disadvantages. Internal consultants have historical and contextual knowledge of the organization that can be very valuable in addressing problems. They also have established long-term relationships and have had many opportunities to build trusting relationships. Internal consultants may be hindered by organization politics and be taken for granted. Since they have to live with the OD interventions they create, they are usually highly invested in their success, although less prone to take risks. An internal consultant might work with a division to create an on-boarding program for new hires, or work with the same division to examine retention issues. External consultants will have less organization insight, and will not be able to see the long term impact of their efforts. Still, they are able to take more risks than internal consultants and enjoy prestige and ready credibility due to their external and novel status. Organizations usually contact external consultants when the consulting expertise needed is not available in-house. An example would be an organization bringing in a consultant who was an expert at diversity issues when the organization lacked such expertise among in-house employees. Table 3.1 lists the pros and cons of being an internal consultant.

Schein (1987) identified three types of consulting roles known as the expert role, the pair-of-hands role, and the collaborator role. The expert role is when the client has neither the time nor interest in dealing with a problem that needs to be fixed. The client hires a consultant and usually gives the consultant authority to fix the issue. For instance, the client might hire you to administer a survey. The pair-of-hands role is also characterized by a client with little time or interest in working on the problem. In this role, the client would bring in a consultant and give directions on what to do such as facilitate a meeting. Schein is not an advocate of either the expert or pair-of-hands role and instead advocates process consulting. Process consulting is based on mutual collaboration between the client and consultant to help the client diagnose its own problems and become independent of the consultant. The collaborative role is very much aligned with contemporary adult learning theory where there is mutuality in determining the needs and resources used in learn-

Table 3.1 Internal Consulting: Pros and Cons

Pros	Cons
• You may be able to take longer gaining entry.	• You are part of the culture you are seeking to change.
• You will probably know the client.	• Your department may have a poor image.
• You may know something about the client's problems.	• You may have a poor image.
• You know the history of the organization.	• You may be imposed upon by the organization.
• You may share the same values.	• You may know things about the client that you can't disclose.
• You may spot non-genuine reasons for calling you in.	• You may have problems over confidentiality.
• You will probably know where to go for more information.	• You may be part of the problem.
• You will be able to find the real client more easily.	• You may have difficulty consulting either above or below your rank.
• You may already have established a good reputation for helping.	• You may have to confront people who might take offense and retaliate.
• You may be able to ask for help from other internal consultants.	• You may be discounted as a prophet in your own land.
• You may find it easier to get involved in implementation and follow-up.	• You may fear that giving bad news could adversely affect your career prospects.

Adapted from: Cockman, Evans & Reynolds (1996).

ing between the educator and learner as elucidated by Burke (1992): "The primary though not exclusive function of OD consultants is to help clients learn how to help themselves more effectively" (p. 174). Block (1999) identifies the characteristics of Schein's three types of consulting which are presented in Table 3.2.

It is often common for an organization to request training to solve problems, casting you as the consultant into the expert role. Yet, very often training does truly address the root cause of the problem. I once had a client who wanted me to create a training curriculum to increase retention of its technicians who were leaving for the competition. They originally hired me as a "pair-of-hands," but I was able to convince them to take a more collaborative approach. After conducting an action research project that involved stakeholder interviews and focus groups with technicians, it became clear that a training curriculum was not an appropriate intervention. Technicians were leaving because they did not see a career ladder in the company. So, instead of a training curriculum, the intervention became

Table 3.2 Comparison of Types of Consulting

Expert	Pair-of-Hands	Collaborator
• Manager plays inactive role. • Consultant makes decisions about how to proceed. • Consultant controls information and intervention. • Technical control rests with the consultant. • Collaboration is not required. • Two-way communication limited. • Consultant's goal is solving immediate problem. • Consultant plans and implements main events. • Manager judges after the fact.	• Consultant assumes passive role. • Consultant follows manager's direction. • Manager selects procedures for data collection and analysis. • Manager decides how to proceed. • Control rests with the manager. • Collaboration is not really necessary. • Two-way communication is limited. • Manager specifies change procedures for the consultant to implement. • Manager evaluates results and judges from a distance. • The consultant's goal is to make the system more effective by the application of specialized knowledge.	• Consultant and manager are interdependent. • Decision making is bilateral. • Data collection and analysis are joint efforts. • Control issues become matters for discussion and negotiation. • Collaboration is considered essential and permeates project. • Communication is Two-way. • Implementation responsibilities are determined by discussion and agreement. • Goal is long-term problem solving—ensuring problems stay solved.

Adapted from Block, P. (1999).

a much more elaborate on-boarding program and effort toward developing the careers of the technicians and retaining them long-term.

Peter Block, one of the most influential scholars of consulting practices, originally wrote the classic *Flawless Consulting* in 1981. In the book he urges consultants to function in Schein's collaborator mode and offers several steps in collaborative consulting:

1. Define initial problem.
2. Decide to proceed.
3. Select dimensions.
4. Decide who to involve.

5.   Select the method.
6.   Collect data.
7.   Funnel the data.
8.   Summarize data.
9.   Analyze data.
10. Present feedback results.
11. Make recommendations.
12. Make decision on actions.

Block suggests there are two requirements for flawless consulting (Block, 1981, 1999): being authentic, and completing the business of each consulting phase. Being authentic involves communicating your experience with the client, leveraging client commitment through communication, and building trust. Authenticity with clients means you are able to explain to them without alienating them how they are being defensive about every suggestion you make and finding a reason it won't work. Being authentic entails finding ways of sharing honest feedback with your clients in a way that saves face. Clients will come to rely on your ability and willingness to identify the "elephant in the room" if you can learn to do it in a tactful and respectful manner. A consultant once worked with a very command-and-control president. Most employees were afraid of him and very affected by his mood. One day she was meeting with him and he was perplexed about how to better motivate his workforce. She looked at him and said, "You know, I think you should just try smiling for a change and see what kind of results you get." The president was furious at the "frivolous" suggestion and threw her out of his office. Nonetheless, after about 3 weeks, the president called the consultant back and told her, "You were right." He could not believe the effect a visible change in his demeanor had on the organization. The consultant in this story risked being authentic with the client, and in the end was able to have a profound influence on him when he realized his effect on the organization.

The other requirement for flawless consulting, completing the business of each phase, means you follow the action research model of contracting, data collection, feedback, implementation, and evaluation. It is your job to push the client to continue moving through the discovery phase until an intervention is decided on and implemented. In addition to identifying the importance of authenticity

Table 3.3 An Overview of Consulting Skills

Technical Skills	Interpersonal Skills	Consulting Skills
Specific to Your Discipline:	Apply to All Situations:	Requirements of Each Consulting Phase:
• Engineering • Project management • Planning • Marketing • Manufacturing • Personnel • Finance • System analysis • Etc.	• Assertiveness • Supportiveness • Confrontation • Listening • Management style • Group process	Contracting • Negotiating wants • Coping with mixed motivation • Dealing with concerns about exposure and the loss of control • Doing triangular and rectangular contracting Diagnosis • Surfacing layers of analysis • Dealing with political climate • Resisting the urge for complete data • Seeing the interview as an intervention Feedback • Funneling data • Identifying and working with different forms of resistance • Presenting personal and organizational data Decision • Running group meetings • Focusing on here and now • Not taking it personally Implementation • Securing commitment

Adapted from Block (1981), p 7.

and helping the client through the full action research process, Block separates consulting skills into three areas to include technical, interpersonal, and consulting. These skills are summarized in Table 3.3.

As a consultant you will generally work at both substantive and affective levels when dealing with clients and making interventions. The substantive level consists of problem solving, rational thinking, and focusing on the technical or business problem. For example, if you are consulting on a reorganization of a customer service department, you will identify current problems with customer service and identify ways the problems might be corrected. Let's say that the customer service response time from complaint to resolution is too long. You would help identify variables that contribute to the length of the process as well as ways of changing the procedures or policies to decrease the time it takes from receipt of a complaint to the resolution of it.

The affective level deals with feelings, relationships, responsibility, trust, and, the consultant's own needs (Block, 1999). In the case of the customer service issue, you will have to address the feelings of the customer service agents. They may be frustrated at structural barriers to doing their job faster, or resistant to making changes in their daily operating procedures. Job roles and responsibilities may need to be renegotiated and the emotional work aspects of their job taken into account.

Ideally you want a mutual relationship with your client. You also have a responsibility to be client-centered by having appropriate technical expertise for the client's problem and interpersonal skills to deal with the client on both individual and group levels. Being a client-centered consultant demands that you sport a wide range of professional and interpersonal skills with sufficient flexibility to deal with a variety of clients and situations. You also need to have a deep understanding of the helping process within the context of your professional discipline. It is also important for you to view the relationship with clients as developmental. As a client-centered consultant, you must be willing to start where your clients are, not where you think they should be. You also need to help them decide what data or information to collect and provide adequate theoretical framing to help them make sense of the data or make sound decisions about courses of action. You also have a responsibility to help the client gain commitment to the selected intervention, and to assist them in implementing the intervention and arranging follow-up if appropriate. Finally, in a client-centered relationship, you have a responsibility to separate from the relationship as soon as possible and ensure that clients retain ownership of the problem and do not become dependent on you.

Consultants exhibit a range of behaviors from non-directive to directive. The more non-directive a consultant you are, the more

Reflector	Process Specialist	Fact Finder	Alternative Identifer	Colaborator (in problem solving)	Trainer or Educator	Technical Specialist	Advocate
Raises questions for reflection	Observes problem solving process and raises issues mirroring feedback	Gathers data and simulates thinking interpretively	Identifies alternatives and resources for client and helps assess consequences	Offers alternatives and participates in decisions	Trains client	Regards links and provides policy or practice decisions	Proposes guidelines, persuades or directs in the problem solving

Adapted from: Lippitt, (1975).

Figure 3.1 Consulting styles

involved your client will be in identifying the root cause of their problem and proposing a solution. Less directive approaches also result in higher degrees of client buy-in to the solution. Less directive approaches will focus on asking the client questions to help stimulate reflection and problem solving on their own. Less directive approaches may require more patience and time. Sometimes, however, a more directive approach may be needed when the client lacks expertise to solve the problem. In such instances you may need to offer specific suggestions for addressing the client's problem. Lippitt and Lippitt (1975) created a continuum to describe consulting roles ranging from non-directive to directive. Directive consultants, according to Lippitt and Lippitt, assume a leadership stance and initiate activities in contrast to the non-directive consultant who merely provides information to clients and leaves it to them to act. Lippitt and Lippitt identified eight roles along their continuum outlined in Figure 3.1.

Consultants also have different styles for dealing with clients. Blake and Mouton (1976; 1983) identified four which were summarized by Cockman et al. (1996): acceptant, catalytic, confrontational, and prescriptive. If you use an acceptant style you tend to help clients by empathic listening and by providing emotional support. This style of neutral, non-judgmental support can help clients to relax their defenses, confront disabling emotional reactions, and find their own way forward. It allows and encourages clients to clear what is blocking their ability to deal logically and rationally with their problem. In many respects it is typical of the early stages of counseling. However, it can also be used in other situations with individuals and groups.

Another style is catalytic. If you prefer this style you are skilled at helping clients gather more data about the problem, analyze it, and decide the relative importance of it. You help the clients make a diagnosis. The catalytic style can use a wide range of data collection techniques. The style intent is to provide data to allow the clients to choose options and solutions. This style is typified at the interpersonal level with questions beginning with who, what, why, when, where, and how. This approach makes this a diagnostic style. Solutions are always generated by the clients.

The confrontational style helps clients by calling attention to discrepancies between the values and beliefs they hold and how they put these values and beliefs into practice. We have theories in our head (espoused theories) and yet behave in ways contrary to them (theories in use). Consultants using this style point out these contradictions so clients can see the discrepancies and decide if they want to change.

The fourth, prescriptive style, usually involves you listening to the clients' problem, collecting the data they require, making sense of data from their own experience, and presenting the clients with a solution or recommendation. It is likely the most common, although probably not the most effective, consulting style applied. This style would also be known as the "expert" approach. It is assumed that the clients do not have the skill, knowledge, or objectivity to effectively diagnose and solve the problem. In reality, this is rarely the case. Consultants can be "experts" without driving the process and knowing when expertise is needed.

TRADITIONAL OD COMPETENCIES

"A consultant is one who provides help, counsel, advice, and support, which implies that such a person is wiser than most people" (Burke, 1992, p. 173). Cummings and Worley (2005) suggest that foundational competencies of OD include an understanding of organizational behavior, individual psychology, group dynamics, management and organization theory, research methods, comparative cultural perspectives, and functional knowledge of business. To their list I have added analysis and negotiation of power relations, in keeping with the critical perspective this book has on the OD process.

In addition to the technical consulting skills outlined above, Burke (1992) identifies important interpersonal competencies that are key to effective consulting. The first is your ability to tolerate ambiguity, since every organization and every problem are unique and will require a customized solution. Another important interpersonal competency is your ability to influence the client. As a consultant, you usually do not have formal organizational power to implement needed changes, making it important that you have well-honed persuasive skills. It is also helpful to possess the ability to confront difficult issues that organization members are reluctant to face. This is never easy, although often pivotal when addressing challenges in the organization and helping it to move toward a change. Your ability to support and nurture others, especially during times of conflict or stress is also imperative and usually includes the ability to listen well and empathize, especially during interviews. Your ability to recognize your feelings and intuitions quickly, distinguish them from the client, and use them when appropriate and timely is also helpful along with the ability to conceptualize and articulate relationships (cause and effect) and linkages within the client system. The consulting role is highly educative, also requiring you to grasp teachable moments with the client and create learning opportunities to enhance the organization's capacity to deal with current and future problems. Consulting work can be challenging and stressful, so maintaining your sense of humor is also a good tension breaker. Finally, Burke advocates that we need to exude self-confidence, interpersonal savvy, and a sense of mission about our work. Burke suggests this sense of mission involves a belief that OD work is worthwhile and potentially helpful to others. The list of OD technical and interpersonal skills is somewhat daunting and requires our vigilance about our own ongoing learning, development, and integrity.

The competencies put forward in this section are fundamental to effective OD practice, yet Wheatley et al. (2003) observe that the term *competencies* is troubling by itself, since competencies may have little value until they are integrated into the being and practice of a person in a holistic fashion. This calls for interconnection between the OD practitioners, the systems in which they work, their values, knowledge, and expertise. The next section attempts to integrate traditional competencies with a critical consulting practice.

CRITICAL CONSULTING

As this chapter has discussed, consulting work takes many forms in many types of organizations. Although the typical image may be of an internal or external corporate consultant in a *Fortune 500* firm, consultants in adult education and HRD can be found in education, nonprofit, government, healthcare, and business. Consultants in these areas do a myriad of things such as evaluate programs, identify new managerial structures, develop boards, create governance plans, conduct needs assessments, engage in coaching, and provide training, just to name a few. Highly developed consulting skills are imperative for people doing developmental and educational work. These skills ensure that you are able to provide the best analysis and services for the stakeholder(s) and that the proposed interventions are sound and ethical. Consulting work is contested, as Burke (1992) observes,

> It is painfully obvious that most organizations treat their most valued resources—employees—as if they were expendable . . . . In the name of efficiency and economic or top management pressure, some people in organizations may be bored, some may be discriminated against, and many may be treated unfairly or inequitably regarding their talent and performance. If OD helps correct these imbalances, it is long overdue, but what about the organization? If it doesn't survive, there will be no jobs, no imbalances to correct. Of the two words represented by OD, practitioners heretofore have spent more time on development than on organization. They are equally important however; if either is out of balance, the OD consultant's goal is to redress the imbalance. (p. 183)

Burke's words capture the ongoing paradox of organization life—tension between individual autonomy and the requirements of the organization. He notes that for us as OD consultants, it is important to understand OD values yet be able to live within the contradictions between our own humanistic values and the productivity-driven demands of organizations. He offers that perhaps a new model of OD is when human needs and effective process receive the most attention, the bottom line will take care of itself. This view is aligned with alternative organization models that focus on health and well-being. Hoque (2007) advocates a social business model for companies seeking to make a difference. "Social businesses have a humanitarian mission but are set up to earn a profit in a model superior to traditional philanthropy because it is self-sustaining" (p. 45). For example, SKS Microfinance is a 9-year old company in India that makes tiny loans to poor people so that they can create or expand small businesses. Hoque emphasizes, "It's not simply deciding to go do good somewhere in the world. It's having a holistic management framework and analytics through which the company can rationally assess such opportunities in the context of the company's mission and strategy, and then act effectively" (p. 46). As Grey and Willmott (2005) observe, performance is not a bad goal, but performative intent is. It is our responsibility as OD consultants to strike a delicate balance between multiple stakeholder needs, including our own. This section proposes how we might accomplish that through critical consulting.

The current business context makes our work as critical consultants even more important. The high profile ethical failures of major corporations and executives have tarnished the image of corporations and management, perhaps for good reason. Several high level executives, usually CEOs or CFOs, have been convicted of crimes and sentenced to long prison terms. The behavior of these organizations and executives is inexcusable. Yet, certainly they did not act alone in proffering deception and wrong-doing. One issue that has yet to be raised is whether or where organization development broke down and allowed these transgressions to occur in the Enrons of the world. Even we can be guilty of creating organizations that do wrong as OD consultants. Certainly education and development of employees (or the lack thereof) played a role in these indiscretions. Perhaps one day those of us responsible for employee and organization development will be held more accountable for our actions or inactions and the failure of learning at the individual and organization levels when it results in such misdeeds against the marginalized. The convictions leveled at the leaders and purse holders were warranted, but also point to where the most value is placed in organizations—the top jobs and finance. This orientation also results from a performative value system. Yet, there is huge accountability on our shoulders in human resources and organization development that plays an equally if not more important role in determining outcomes. Further, if a systems view is adopted, one must acknowledge that the organization system itself broke down in these instances, including OD efforts. A more critical approach to OD and the consulting process may help us make more ethical and sustainable decisions for all stakeholders.

As recent transgressions indicate, there is a need for OD professionals to help instill a sense of social responsibility in their organizations. Yet, a recent study (Fenwick & Bierema, 2008) showed that HR professionals in organizations with explicit commitments to corporate social responsibility (CSR) did not regard advancing their companies' commitment to social responsibility as within their purview. The researchers concluded that there is much work to be accomplished in helping the human resource and organization development field view social responsibility and sustainability as relevant organization initiatives for their attention. The Fenwick and Bierema study underscores the need for us to take a more critical, mindful approach to our work. A more optimistic view of HR's role in social responsibility is promoted by Lockwood (2004) who suggests that OD leaders who are strategically implementing CSR programs have demonstrated return on investment, taken a role in promoting organization ethics, and built management and human capital into key business transactions. She reports that 63% of HR departments are spending on learning and training initiatives related to CSR, 40% are changing company policy in response to environmental issues, 36% are changing company policy in response to grassroots pressure to change certain business practices, and 32%

are increasing involvement in social programs. She suggests that OD leaders can influence three primary standards of CSR—ethics, employment practices, and community involvement.

It is assumed that as a critical consultant you possess the traditional competencies outlined in previous sections of this chapter and that you have sound training in the theory and practice of OD. In addition to these competencies critical OD consultants:

- Serve as stewards of organization well-being and social responsibility.
- Advocate for stakeholder interests.
- Interrogate reality.
- Work as tempered radicals for change ranging from awareness to activism.

The following sections speak to our unique roles as critical consultants.

Stewardship of Organization Well-being and Social Responsibility

This book defines OD as an intentional, systemic process of facilitating change to improve an organization's well-being. Well-being is a holistic approach to promoting organization health that considers factors beyond simple profit and productivity. As critical consultants, we are committed to helping organizations attain higher levels of well-being in their efforts to conduct OD and make interventions.

Many professionals are attracted to adult education and HRD careers because they are oriented toward developing others. Yet, learning and development within any context are bound to span the range from exhilarating to taxing to toxic, particularly in organizations under pressure to perform. Promoting organization well-being is a challenging task that can have deleterious effects on us, its practitioners. Promoting well-being in the organization includes promoting well-being within ourselves as well.

OD work is emotion-laden and Goldman Schuyler (2004) suggests those of us who serve as buffers between management and workers are at risk of becoming "toxic handlers." A toxic handler is "a manager who voluntarily shoulders the sadness, frustration, bitterness, and anger that are endemic to organizational life" (Frost & Robinson, 1999, p. 98). In OD we often find ourselves working with employees to make changes they find difficult or threatening such as modifying jobs to significant restructuring. Frost and Robinson view the presence of toxic handlers as a necessary evil in organizations, especially those characterized by high levels of creative and strategic work. Toxic handlers are at risk of burnout, stress, and physical illness. Goldman Schuyler's own poignant account of becoming ill after engaging in toxic handling is a testament to the documented effects of its damage to the immune system. Drawing on Frost and Schein, Goldman Schuyler (2004) observes, "one must learn how to spend considerable time immersed in unhealthy environments without being influenced by them in negative ways" (p. 30). Training and organization change initiatives affect workers and the "toxic handlers" assigned to facilitate and manage such work.

> A person attempting to catalyze change needs to sustain their own well-being at deep levels . . . Unless organizational development consultants increase their ability to manage their deeper levels of health, they risk becoming "toxic handlers" who assist an organization in being healthy by channeling toxicity, rather than by helping it to transform itself in significant ways. (pp. 28-29)

Goldman Schuyler (2004) advocates that we as organizational practitioners are most effective when the change process includes: (1) skills in organizational change and business; (2) a model for organizational health; and (3) practical, theoretical approaches for maintaining individual health (encompassing physical, spiritual, and mental well-being). Our goal is to help leaders attend to vision, teamwork, and individual development. It is also important to make sure the organization is providing resources for workers who are grappling with the changes themselves. As critical OD consultants, we play an important role in pursuing organization well-being, but must be aware that the work can be taxing, particularly on ourselves.

Advocacy of Stakeholder Interests and Social Justice

In addition to advocating for organization well-being, critical consultants advocate for stakeholders. The current environment is seeing pressure for organizations to be socially responsible, sustainable, and ethical. OD is increasingly being called on to support these goals through well-managed programs, policies, and practices (Lockwood, 2004). OD is also engaging the organization and its stakeholders around issues of sustainability and organization well-being. Lockwood suggests that OD can communicate the value of CSR through communications, employee relations, health, safety, and community relations.

The principle of social justice may take many forms. It requires the consultant to consider all stakeholders and consider "who benefits?" from the OD intervention. Cervero and Wilson (2006) eloquently describe how competing interests and asymmetrical power relations can be negotiated. Dedication to social justice also assumes a wider commitment to redistributing power in society. This means that we also need to consider how OD interventions will affect groups in the organization that have been historically marginalized due to class, race, gender, sexual orientation, religion, ethnicity, or other positionalities, and how the organization's actions will affect the wider community.

Interrogate Reality

Scott's (2004) book *Fierce Conversation,* outlines powerful principles for becoming an authentic and provocative communicator. One of the principles she advocates is the ability to interrogate reality, or expose the distance between the status quo and desired outcome. This is a challenging order as it can be very difficult to accurately articulate reality. U.S. automotive manufacturers are a good example. They have never been savvy about defining what consumers want (fuel efficient cars) until a crisis occurs such as escalating gas prices and global warming, and it is too late to meet demand. If automotive manufacturers were better at interrogating reality, they would not be performing so poorly in the market, especially as compared to other automotive companies from Japan who anticipated demand for fuel economy in the 1980s and again in the 2000s. Interrogating reality is similar to what Block (1982, 1999) calls authenticity. "Authentic behavior with a client means you put into words what you are experiencing with the client as you work. *This is the most powerful thing you can do to have the leverage you are looking for and to build client commitment"* (p. 37). More information about interrogating reality will be shared in Chapter 6.

Work as Tempered Radicals for Change
Ranging from Awareness to Activism

One means of moderating the contested role of serving multiple stakeholders, being a toxic handler, and sometimes finding ourselves at odds with organization values is through tempered radicalism (Meyerson, 2004). Tempered radicals, or those Meyerson (2004) refers to as "not quite a full-fledged radical" (p. 14) or "under the radar rebels" (p. 16) act for social change within their organizations. Meyerson explains that tempered radicals:

> Engage in small battles, at times operating so quietly that they may not surface on the cultural radar as "rebels." By pushing back on conventions, they create opportunities for change within their organizations. They are not heroic leaders of revolutionary action; rather, they are cautious and committed catalysts who slowly make a difference. (p. 16)

As critical OD consultants, we can use tempered radicalism from simply raising awareness about issues to outright activism for change in the organization. Meyerson and colleague Scully have conducted research on tempered radicals for the past 20 years, interviewing over 200 professionals who self-identified as change agents. They suggest that tempered radicals operate on a "fault line" and that they are organizational insiders who are usually successful at their careers. These individuals mitigate their desire to advance their change agenda while simultaneously fitting into the dominant corporate culture. Tempered radicalism is an ideal strategy for us as OD consultants as we live on the fault line described by Meyerson and Scully.

Tempered radicals have impact through "little acts of self expression—their dress, language or leadership style" (Meyerson, 2004, p. 17). Their small actions can have a rippling effect in the organization or what Karl Weick has termed "deviation amplification" (in Meyerson, 2004), or when a single unusual action paves the way for other acts to follow. Meyerson urges that tempered radicals are persistent and patient, willing to take small steps toward their goal. This can be accomplished by what she terms "leveraging small wins" (p. 17). A small win was the consultant described earlier who got her client to smile. This small change was a major revelation to her about how several things add up to create an organization culture. Another example of a small win at my university was the LGBTQ organization's distribution of stickers that said "safe place" indicating faculty and staff who completed an awareness training about LGBTQ issues on campus. These stickers have begun appearing all over campus, helping to raise awareness about homosexual issues and identifying allies. Other more significant changes have occurred including stronger institutional support for partner benefits and a climate survey.

> The key assumption underlying tempered radicalism is that organizations are continually evolving, adapting to market conditions, workforce requirements, and technological innovations. Sometimes the changes are dramatic, but most often they take the form of incremental adjustments. Tempered radicals push and prod the system through a variety of subtle processes, rechanneling information and opportunities, questioning assumptions, changing boundaries of inclusion, and scoring small wins. (Meyerson, 2004, pp. 17-18)

Although Meyerson and Fletcher (2000) advocate finding other like-minded individuals when pursuing small wins, it is not required, and many tempered radicals operate solo by taking localized change and creating more systematic shifts.

> Tempered radicals bear no banners; they sound no trumpets. Their ends are sweeping, but their means are mundane. They are firm in their commitments, yet flexible in the ways they

fulfill them. Their actions may be small but can spread like a virus. They yearn for rapid change but trust in patience. They often work individually yet pull people together. Instead of stridently pressing their agendas, they start conversations. Rather than battling powerful foes, they seek powerful friends. And in the face of setbacks, they keep going. To do all this, tempered radicals understand revolutionary change for what it is—a phenomenon that can occur suddenly but more often than not requires time, commitment, and the patience to endure. (Meyerson, 2001, p. 100)

Our work in OD is always working for change. Sometimes it comes more easily than others. Because we operate on a fault line between employees and management, we often find ourselves needing to work as tempered radicals aiming for small wins in order to serve multiple and sometimes conflicting needs of stakeholders. Chapter 6 will profile critical interventions and offer more suggestions for how we can function as tempered radicals.

SUMMARY

Focused on the OD consultant, this chapter defined the OD consultant and types of consulting. The chapter identified traditional OD competencies and skills and styles in the consulting process. In addition to traditional OD consulting competencies, critical OD consultants serve as stewards of organization well-being and social responsibility. They advocate for stakeholder interests, interrogate reality, and work as tempered radicals.

CHAPTER 4

Stakeholders and Socially Responsible Practice

Organization development occurs on a fault line where we, as consultants, are expected to satisfy management while simultaneously serving employees. That may mean implementing a change that causes significant employee angst, or coaching employees to raise issues that management may not want to hear. The expectations of these two stakeholder groups may be contradictory, leaving us in a no-win situation where personal ethical principles must be abandoned in order to achieve managerial expectations (Marsick, 1997). This pressure may also force us to be less attuned to other stakeholders within the context who are either directly or indirectly affected by the OD initiative. Korten (1996) observed in a speech to the Academy of Human Resource Development Conference that there is a "serious disconnect between your own values and the realities of life in many of the corporations in which you work" (p. 1). Korten's point underscores the paradoxical nature of OD work, although this inconsistency is not broadly discussed. Yet, it is very important for us to have a keen awareness of the stakeholders in the OD process, the skill to navigate the politics of organization life with savvy, the tact to raise challenging issues on behalf of stakeholders, and the attention to our own self-preservation when needed. By acknowledging and discussing this contradictory state of affairs we can learn how to address multiple, conflicting needs in a way that creates better outcomes for all stakeholders and reinforce the importance of doing representative and responsible OD work that doesn't put us out of work.

Traditional OD theory and practice tend to align with managerial and organization interests, making managers and stockholders favored participants in the process at the expense of less powerful and obvious stakeholders such as employees or communities.

This chapter focuses on stakeholders in the OD process. A key feature of the framework for this book is to understand the multiple and conflicting interests that we as OD consultants serve. Appreciating this paradox involves considering and accommodating multiple stakeholders including the obvious clients (management and employees) as well as the not-so-obvious stakeholders such as customers, communities, and the environment. A stakeholder orientation differs from a shareholder perspective, yet, much of OD theory and practice assumes that a managerialist, stockholder-driven orientation is normal, neutral, and beneficial. As a critical, reflective, representative, and responsible OD consultant, it is imperative to consider how *all* stakeholders are impacted by OD.

This chapter defines the stakeholder as part of the book's framework for understanding the consultant, stakeholder, context, and interventions using a critical OD perspective. This chapter identifies stakeholders, defines the OD client, advocates process consulting as a stakeholder-centered practice, introduces the concept of positionality, underscores the importance of negotiating stakeholder needs, considers what OD outcomes matter to stakeholders, and finally, advocates for a socially representative and responsible OD practice.

IDENTIFYING THE STAKEHOLDERS

There are two different types of orientations in organization work with regard to outcomes. The prevailing stockholder orientation is performative, placing value on economics and performance, only considering social responsibility when it is profitable or required by law. The stockholder orientation privileges managerial and organizational interests:

> A corporation is the private property of its stockholders and exists to create wealth and provide goods and services to the market. While obligated to comply with legal constraints, its primary goal is profitability; only secondarily is it to be concerned with goals, policies and strategies aimed at serving the needs of external publics. (Acar, Aupperle, & Lowy, 2001, p. 29)

A stockholder OD intervention may adopt a new manufacturing procedure or work process that saves money, even if it makes the worker's life more difficult or unpleasant. The profit potential trumps the human concern in this perspective. Alternatively, the stakeholder orientation argues for broader organizational accountability to affected stakeholders. This orientation would not impose a change that only benefited the bottom line, but would be more participative by consulting with affected parties before making a change. A stakeholder orientation is usually compromise minded, because there are more interests at stake. Freeman (1984) describes stakeholders as "any group or individual who can affect or is affected by the achievement of the organization's objectives" (p. 46). Using Ackoff's (1974) "vested interests" perspective and Freeman's (1984) notion of corporate impact, Acar et al. define "stakeholder" as "a corporation [that] exists by permission of society and, as such, is the servant of external stakeholder groups" (p. 29). They note that most organizations fall along a continuum between stockholder and stakeholder orientation making defining social responsibility fairly ambiguous. Clarkson (1995) defines primary stakeholders as those on whom a corporation depends for its survival such as shareholders, investors, employees, customers, and suppliers. Clarkson defines secondary stakeholders as those who are influenced or affected by the organization but not engaged in transactions that are essential to the organization's survival.

Potential stakeholders in OD may include the client(s), organization, employees, management, community, environment, suppliers, and others. A stakeholder perspective acknowledges that addressing multiple, sometimes conflicting needs is a process of negotiation in OD where power relations play out among different groups with varying degrees of power. A critical OD recognizes and values multiple stakeholders and seeks outcomes that matter for *all* parties.

Senge, Smith, Kruschwitz, Laur, and Schley (2008) suggest that we are moving from shareholder value that depends on cost risk and reduction, reputation and legitimacy, growth, and innovation and repositioning, to organizations that create sustainable value through product stewardship, pollution prevention, clean technology, and a sustainability vision. They recognize "civil society stakeholders" in the model. Seventh Generation, manufacturer of green household and personal care products, is a stakeholder-oriented company that has grown to over $100 million in sales while remaining true to its mission of "educating 'this and future generations' about their impact on 'our health and the health of the environment'" (Senge et al., 2008, p. 328). Simply buying their products provides a mini-sustainability lesson. Educational information is on the package. They partnered with Greenpeace to try an experiment. Instead of an advertising campaign, they sponsored an environmental training program titled Change It. The goal was to interact with stakeholders in an alternative way from purchasing their product. They replaced normal promotional materials in their stores with information on making a positive impact in the world by encouraging nominations of youth to participate in the program. Long term analysis of the program is not available, but Seventh Generation had more retailers seeking participation in the program than when they were giving away washing machines (Senge et al, 2008).

The retailer Costco is another example of a company that puts stakeholders first, even with pressure from Wall Street to be less employee and customer oriented. Their founder and CEO, Jim Sinegal, is highly visible and accessible, donning a nametag that says only "Jim," answering his own telephone, sending his own faxes, and making only $350,000 per year (a very small salary when compared to other CEO's multimillion dollar compensation packages). At one page, he has the shortest CEO contract on record that says he can be terminated for cause. Employees are paid a living wage that is 40% higher than Sam's Club (a similar retailer owned by Wal-Mart). Over 90% of employees receive better-than-average benefits and health insurance (Goldberg & Ritter, 2006). Costco's practices have earned it a loyal employee and customer base. Most Costco workers have been with the company since its founding in 1983, where almost 100% of promotions are from within. The company is the fourth largest retailer. Sinegal acknowledges that paying high wages bucks conventional wisdom, but pays little attention to Wall Street analysts urging him to pay workers less to enhance profitability. "Wall Street is in the business of making money between now and next Tuesday. We're in the business of building an organization, an institution that we hope will be here 50 years from now. And paying good wages and keeping your people working with you is very good business" (Goldberg & Ritter, 2006). Goldberg and Ritter observe that Sinegal has proven that a company doesn't have to be ruthless to make money. Being humane and ethical also pays and creates high loyalty among stakehoders.

OD consultants can help organizations identify and include stakeholders in the OD process. The first step is actually identifying the organization client, who is a very important stakeholder in the OD process.

IDENTIFYING THE CLIENT

Although it may seem obvious, determining *who the OD client is* can be tricky. The client is any individual or group who needs some kind of help from outside (the consultant) to work on a problem. The client is likely someone with whom the consulting relationship is temporary—although some OD consultancies can last for months or years. Clients also tend to enter the relationship with the consultant on a voluntary basis (Cockman, Evans, & Reynolds, 1996). The client may not be the person who invited the consultant into the organization to contract for OD services. Schein (1987) categorized clients as *contact clients* (the person who initiates the relationship with the consultant), *intermediate clients* (individuals involved in the early stages of the OD process), *primary clients* (those who own the problem for which help is sought), and *ultimate clients* (stakeholders whose welfare and interests may be impacted by the planning and intervention). Sometimes the type of client is not immediately clear and it can take some investigation to identify the primary client. You may find that you have more than one client, or that there is a whole client system and or that it is challenging to identify the primary client.

Revans (1980) suggests that important stakeholders in the process include the person who knows about the problem or has other information useful in its diagnosis. This is often the worker doing the actual task or job. Another important stakeholder is the person who cares about solving the problem. This could be the owner of the problem, and others affected by it. Finally, Revans suggests we need to know who can do something about the solution. People must have authority to act in resolving the issue. It is important to have all of these viewpoints represented in the OD process.

Let's say you are called by a nonprofit professional association to provide some training to a group of members who are being groomed for future leadership roles. Initially, it may seem that your primary client is the education manager who called you to set up the training session. Once you visit the organization and learn more about the project, you begin to understand that the executive director and the president of the organization are the primary clients, because they are funding the program and have the most to gain or lose depending on the success of the program. The program participants are also important clients as they will be directly affected by the program.

Determining "who is the client?" should be accomplished during the contracting period. It may require savvy questioning and keen observation to identify the primary client. You will also want to consider all other clients (contact, intermediate, and ultimate) as important stakeholders in the process, and advocate to represent their interests as appropriate. In the example of the nonprofit leadership training, other affected stakeholders include the public and members of the profession.

PROCESS CONSULTING

Schein (1988) advanced a model of process consulting where you enter into a collaborative role with the client to work through the entire consulting process. Process consulting is of particular import when conducting stakeholder-oriented OD since its underlying value is one of collaboration and mutuality. Collaboration viewed in its broadest sense engages all stakeholder interests in the process. Schein defines process consulting (PC) as:

> PC is a set of activities on the part of the consultant that help the client to perceive, understand, and act upon the process events that occur in the client's environment in order to improve the situation as defined by the client. (Schein, 1988, p. 11, italics in original)

Schein outlined the underlying assumptions of process consulting to include:

1. Clients often do not know what is wrong and need help diagnosing problems.
2. Clients often do not know what services consultants can offer them and need help knowing what type of assistance to seek.
3. Most clients have constructive intentions to improve matters, but need help with identifying what to improve and how to do it.
4. Most organizations will be more effective if they learn how to diagnose and manage their own strengths and weaknesses (no organization is perfect—all have weaknesses).
5. Most consultants cannot learn enough or know enough about the organization and culture to suggest reliable courses of action. Thus, they must partner with the client to identify problems and remedies.
6. Unless the clients learn to see the problem for themselves and think through the remedy, they will not be willing or able to implement solutions and will not learn how to fix future problems. The process consultant can pose alternatives, but the decision making authority must remain in the clients' hands.
7. The essential skill of the process consultant is educative: to pass on the skill of how to diagnose and fix organizational problems to the client.

Consultants specialize in making interventions that are usually change- or learning-oriented. Change interventions involve changes to organization structure, policy, or procedure. Learning interventions can be structural or interpersonal.

POSITIONALITY

Identifying stakeholders and the client using a process consulting approach is an important element of critical consulting. It is also crucial to consider how positionality impacts the relationships and interactions during the consulting process. Organizations are increasingly diverse and the concept of *positionality* has received significant attention in adult education, along with the recognition that context is a significant factor in learning. Context will be further introduced in Chapter 5. Positionality is introduced here, since it is a key variable among stakeholders. Positionality is the way "people are defined not in terms of fixed identities, but by their location within shifting networks of relationships, which can be analyzed and changed" (Maher & Tetreault, 1994, p. 164). Positionality refers to both visible and invisible markers such as ableness, age, class, culture, gender, race, religion, sexual orientation, and so forth. Positionality is "a concept that acknowledges that we are all raced, classed, and gendered, and that these identities are relational, complex, and fluid positions rather than essential qualities" (Martin & Van Gunten, 2002, p. 46). Some aspects of my positionality include that I am a white, female, Midwestern U.S. citizen, who is heterosexual, middle class, and well-educated. These aspects of my being affect how I engage with the world, and how the world engages with me.

We all live framed by socially constructed positions, wanted or not. Positionality shapes how people relate to each other and is deeply implanted in our psyche and culture. Organizations are made up of people who have relationships and use those relationships to accomplish tasks and goals. The success of individuals, groups, or the organization depends on interactions within context and negotiation over competing interests between stakeholders. For instance, organizations are structured to privilege individuals who hold managerial positions, who tend to be white males. Often the managers are expected to have answers to problems. There are many cases of management failing to ask the very workers who have deep knowledge about the business and how the problems might be solved, based on a power relationship that has been created by the organization structure. The managers have assumed their "position" of authority, and the workers have learned their "position" which may be to not speak up or to wait for management to figure it out. When those in power are a dominant group, such as white males, they may not recognize how organization practices and policies prevent women and people of color from advancing or having a voice. This might play out in identifying other white males for promotional opportunities, and overlooking other equally qualified employees who do not fit the stereotype of management. These type of positionality-based dynamics often hurt the organization as a whole by causing problems to remain unsolved and by not developing the workforce to its full potential.

Although OD and HRD recognize diversity and articulate its importance through their discourse, it is less prominent in practice. Further, positionality is not a concept that appears in mainstream OD or HRD discourse. Critical and feminist analyses are interested in power relations in organizations which include how voices are privileged or silenced. Such dynamics are good indicators of who is heard, whose interests are advanced, and who is in power. Positionality is directly related to power in organizations. Power has been defined as the ability to impose one's will on others, even amid resistance. More positive definitions of power assume that it is the ability to influence others or to bring about change. The exercise of power happens through relationships. All individuals have some degree of power, although it may be equal or unequal, stable, shifting, or changing. Power takes various forms and is fluid, shifting depending on place and positionality.

To gain a better understanding of how OD is addressing issues of positionality and power, a review of the indexes of widely popular OD textbooks *Organization Development and Change* by Cummings and Worley (2005), and *Organization Development: Behavioral Science Interventions for Organization Improvement by* French and Bell (1999) was conducted. Gender, race, and diversity receive little or no mention. Power is discussed, although usually in the sense of types of power (charismatic, positional, etc.) or conditions of use. In Cummings and Worley's (2005) comprehensive OD textbook, women are indexed on 6 pages of this 694-page volume. Race is noted 0 times, diversity is documented 7 times, and power is mentioned 5 times. The factors of women, race, or diversity do not even appear in French and Bell's (1999) 343-page text. Despite this oversight, the French and Bell text has the most comprehensive chapter on power and politics in an OD textbook and they acknowledge "organization development has been criticized for not taking into account power in organizations" (p. 282). Although they indicate that there has recently been an "outpouring of theory and research on power and politics" (p. 282), they concede that OD is still in the early stages of understanding how to relate power to OD. Their chapter begins to address the little understood role of power in OD. These omissions of less privileged stakeholders from the discourse parallel the findings of a study I co-authored on the Proceedings of the AHRD (Academy of Human Resource Development) Conference over a 5-year period (Bierema & Cseh, 2003). This feminist review of over 600 proceedings submissions showed that very little research is actually being conducted on issues of diversity in HRD. The lack of discussion and study of these issues by fields that have historically claimed humanistic, person-centered values presents a problematic contradiction between espoused values and reality. Both OD and HRD can look to the work in adult education on positionality and power to inform thinking and practice as related to diverse and multicultural organizations.

If, as an OD consultant, you wish to impact inequities in organizations and attend to issues of diversity and multiculturalism, it behooves you to reflect not only on how positionality shapes the overall OD process, but also on how your own positionality shapes your values, beliefs, and actions as a consultant. The concept of positionality has led many scholars in adult higher education to examine their own *positions*. One might call such examinations *critical reflections* based on outcomes that lead to better understandings of one's practices (Brookfield, 1990; Johnson-Bailey & Cervero, 2000; Tisdell, 1995, 2001).

Positionality influences people's life and work experiences. Depending on what social positions people belong to, they experience treatment differently from others, either better or worse. Unfortunately, during the OD process, key positionalities may go unrecognized or unheard. It is not easy to engage in a dialogue on sensitive issues about how organization practices may be impacting people based on class, race, ethnicity, gender, or sexual orientation. Yet, these issues may hold the key to addressing the problems OD seeks to remedy.

As OD consultants, we have a unique positionality. We are in a marginal power position by virtue of the consulting role that possesses little, if any, official organization power. We are often regarded as experts and outsiders to the client (even if we are internal consultants) which usually allows us certain degrees of freedom. To be effective we also have to rely on our interpersonal skills and

1. Reflect on your positionality in life. What are the key visible and invisible markers of your positionality? Write them down. These may include things like race, gender, age, ethnicity, sexual orientation, ableness, religion, education, and so forth.

2. Next, identify at least three ways you believe your positionality impacts your work in OD.

3. Next, identify at least three ways that your positionality impacts how clients work with you.

Figure 4.1 Positionality exercise for OD consultants

authentic behaviors. These help us build trust and a relationship with the client that gives us power and influence. Yet, our unique positionality, such as gender and race, may cause the client to be less receptive to us. A black female consultant may have a more difficult time gaining entry and receiving equal compensation to a white male consultant, or white males in the organization may not view her as qualified or competent to complete the OD process. Women or people of color advocating for diversity may be viewed as "having an agenda" and viewed with suspicion much more than a white male advocating for the same goals.

Chapter 3 advocated self-knowledge and development for all consultants. Engaging in work around your own positionality is vital in working with stakeholders. The above exercise depicted in Figure 4.1 helps you consider how positionality plays out in your life and work. As you work on it, remember that positionality can bring you advantage, disadvantage, or neutral effects and it will change depending upon the situation and environmental context in which you are working. To that end, it is often most helpful to place yourself within a particular context as you answer the questions in the exercise.

Many OD texts and theories assume that the OD process is governed by neutrality and rationality, conducted by consultants whose gender and race are invisible. These texts disregard power relations and how they shape the OD process. Yet, positionality can influence the OD process in myriad ways. Stakeholders all have positionality and these multiple positionalities intersect and influence the OD process. An awareness of positionality throughout the process helps you represent the interests of a range of stakeholders including the client, affected workers, affected customers, affected community, and yourself.

NEGOTIATING STAKEHOLDER NEEDS

With positionality comes a set of values and needs that are usually sought when negotiating interests in organizations. It is important to acknowledge that all parties involved in an OD process have interests and needs. It is human nature that stakeholders will work to protect and achieve their individual interests. The interests may be specific to the OD intervention ("I want to convince the organization to use intervention X"); or they may be more instrumental ("Through the intervention, I want to secure a promotion, establish credibility, or achieve a broader outcome. . . .").

Since there is a dearth of resources in OD to consider how positionality and power shape the process, we will rely on the educational program planning principles set forth by Cervero and Wilson (2006) for insight as to preserving stakeholder interests in the OD process. Cervero and Wilson advocate that processes such as OD are conducted by people who are social and political actors. Throughout the OD process stakeholders make practical judgments about problem definition, important data, interventions, stakeholders, and assessment. Some stakeholders may not even be represented in the process (the community or environment for example), making it important that we and other primary stakeholders recognize their interests and advocate on their behalf. Cervero and Wilson argue that practical judgments are causally connected to the interests of OD consultants and stakeholders who are making decisions and taking action with the goal of creating change and making the current state different. Planning OD programs allows stakeholders to advance their own interests, which is something that matters to all stakeholders. When interests are competing, parties must negotiate to protect their interests. Cervero and Wilson suggest that these dynamics matter because when an OD problem is articulated and an intervention selected, it is essentially a statement of how the world

should be different. At issue, of course, is how the various stakeholder interests are represented during the process. Usually those
with the most power see their interests most privileged. This is why
it is so important to be alert to positionality, because otherwise OD
will perpetuate inequality and oppression.

Cervero and Wilson make three assumptions about practice in
adult education that can be applied to OD. First, there is a reciprocal
relationship between power and OD that is present in all contexts of
practice. We must recognize that the OD process may provide advantages to particular people and disadvantages to others. Consequently, issues relating to "social, economic, cultural, political, racial, and gendered power relations that structure all action in the
world are played out in adult education" (Cervero & Wilson, 2001,
p. 10). Second, the OD process is a site for the struggle of knowledge and power that mimics the larger social context. With this assumption, OD practitioners must recognize the multiple interests of
all stakeholders with attention to conflicting agendas regarding the
production and reproduction of knowledge and power. Finally,
Cervero and Wilson stress that all adult educators are social *activists*. If we apply their logic to OD, that would mean that we as OD
consultants are activists as well. Simply by determining who will
benefit from an initiative, we are already making politically and
ethically grounded decisions that impact stakeholders, even before
data are collected or analyzed.

When negotiating stakeholder interests, Cervero and Wilson
(2001) consider the four variables of power, interests, negotiation,
and responsibility as key dynamics. They define power as the socially structured capacity to act and consider the interpersonal interactions that happen during the OD process as exercises of power
that can either support or constrain action and eventual outcomes.
When power is exercised, it is usually contingent on advancing an
interest or interests. Cervero and Wilson describe interests as being
at the center of agency. Interests may be grounded in values, beliefs, goals, practices, hopes, or expectations, and they drive people
to act in one direction or another. Predictably, interests of the stakeholders do not necessarily match and may be in competition with
one another. Interests direct OD processes and may include things

like quality levels, competition for resources, performance capability, customer satisfaction, interpersonal relationships, working conditions, individual or unit stature, or culture. All OD interventions are causally related to interests of consultants and other planners. Cervero and Wilson identify the process of negotiation as the characteristic activity of planning OD. Negotiation happens with one's own interests and power as well as between interests and power. OD consultants negotiate power relationships, negotiate about power relationships, act in and on social contexts. The pivotal question to ask when negotiating OD is "who benefits?"

CREATING OUTCOMES THAT MATTER
TO STAKEHOLDERS

OD is an empirical process concerned with identifying and diagnosing problems in organizations and then proposing interventions to address the problem. Evaluation is an important aspect of the action research model and OD process, yet, sometimes the outcomes sought may be of little consequence to stakeholders. A stakeholder-orientation demands that OD secure outcomes that matter to and improve the quality of life for stakeholders. This means that OD benefits the overall *well-being* of the organization, not just the bottom line. Good health is generally not defined as the absence of disease, but rather the prevention of it and attainment of vibrant health of the patient. Medicine is successful when its patients have a high quality of life and good health, and satisfaction with their life. Similarly, strong organizations are not merely those with an absence of problems. Organization health or well-being is a measure of how well problems are prevented and opportunities are embraced, and how healthy the overall environment is so that it promotes a high quality of worklife. Activities that enhance organization health and well-being are the ones that matter most for the stakeholders of the organization.

Stakeholder-oriented outcomes that matter in organizations strive to improve the quality of life for all affected parties. This means that rather than simply seeking to reduce a number such as absenteeism or turnover rates, the OD intervention creates an outcome that results in improving the quality of conditions at work for the employees so that they want to come to work or remain at the organization. This approach values both valid and relevant interventions. Valid in the sense that there is prevailing evidence that they work, and relevant in the sense that the intervention results in an outcome that stakeholders care about. Stakeholder-oriented outcomes are not out to simply change a metric, but rather to shift the quality of life in the organization. In the long run, the quality of the intervention and work climate matters more to stakeholders than mere performance statistics. A stakeholder-oriented outcome that matters in OD might be applying dialogical conversation techniques to help solve problems more quickly with less emotion.

SOCIALLY RESPONSIBLE OD

Corporate social responsibility (CSR) movements have become increasingly popular in the wake of corporate scandals. Research on social responsibility in organizations is traceable to the 1950s (Acar et al., 2001), but the issue is receiving increased traction due to a spate of corporate transgressions that have had traumatic consequences for many stakeholders. Adopting a socially responsible stance is an important value when attempting to incorporate stakeholder interests into OD practice.

Social consciousness in organizations is also referred to as social responsibility, corporate social responsibility, corporate social performance, ethics, and organizational social responsibility. Corporate social responsibility is the obligation of the firm to use its resources in ways to benefit society, through committed participation as a member of society, taking into account society at large, and improving welfare of society at large independently of direct gains of the company (Stahl & Grigsby, 2001, p. 287). "Business Impact" (2000, p. 1.02, cited in Moir, 2001) describes corporate social responsibility (CSR) as based on: treating employees fairly and equitably; operating ethically and with integrity; respecting basic human rights; sustaining the environment for future generations; and being a caring neighbor in their communities.

The notion of corporate social performance (CSP) originally derived from an economic framework based on the belief that social responsibility yields financial gain. It has evolved into a more moralistic quest that emphasizes duty. Swanson (1995) explains that whether the CSP was oriented toward economics or morals, both views focus on the logic of individual versus social choice.

Corporate social responsibility (CSR) has come to refer to Carroll's (1999) four categories of economic, legal, ethical and discretionary responsibilities. *Economic responsibilities* refer to the traditional function of business as a provider of products and services and a producer of profits. Profit generation is its most important responsibility. *Legal responsibilities are* compliance with governmental rules and regulations. *Ethical responsibilities* include societal defined expectations that are not dictated by formal law. This is where issues of fairness and justice come into play. An example of ethical behavior would be recalling defective products or spending money to ensure quality control. *Discretionary responsibilities* are voluntary and philanthropic. Often these are expected by society. Examples include Bill Gates's and Ted Turner's philanthropic gestures of offering huge sums of money to fund nonprofit organizations and to promote social justice.

Acar et al. (2001) describe how historically the concept of social responsibility has been conceptualized and researched only in the business context. They make an important contribution in originating the term *organization social responsibility* (OSR) as a broader, more encompassing process than *corporate social performance* (CSP). They explored how a continuum of organizational types from for-profit to not-for-profit value their economic versus social orientation. Although they considered social responsibility based on organization type, they note that nonprofits are also faced with the dilemma of balancing economic and social concerns. Not surprisingly they found that not-for-profits registered higher CSR scores than for-profits at a very high level of statistical significance. They conclude that business still places a greater emphasis on economic concerns and that total social responsibility increases with the move toward not-for-profit.

I contend that it is our responsibility as critical OD consultants not only to function with a high level of social consciousness, but also to educate the organization so that it becomes more socially conscious and responsible in its management practices. Bierema and D'Abundo (2004) offered a definition of socially conscious

HRD that offers guidance to being a social responsibility advocate:

> Socially Conscious human resource development serves an educative and supportive role to help organizations use their resources to benefit their stakeholders. This includes but is not limited to: upholding implied contracts and expectations of the organization, promoting ethical management and leadership, advocating for stakeholders, broadening definitions and measures of organization performance, challenging and revising socially "unconscious" policies and practices, analyzing and negotiating power relations, and promoting the use of organization resources to create social benefit and improve social welfare. (p. 449)

Bierema and D'Abundo argue that developing social consciousness is a learning proposition that is a natural fit with OD's tradition of growth and learning. Practicing OD with social responsibility means negotiating for stakeholder interests. Upholding implied contracts and expectations assumes that organizations create outcomes that fulfill the informal, unwritten expectation that workers will be respected and retained if the organization is to expect their loyalty. The promotion of ethical management and leadership implies that management will function with integrity and a high degree of ethical conduct. Another aspect of social responsibility is advocating for stakeholders in a democratic process as this chapter has discussed extensively. Developing broader definitions and measures of performance is aligned with generating outcomes that matter to stakeholders that go beyond performative profit- and productivity-based metrics. Socially responsible OD involves challenging policies and practices that disenfranchise others, such as a promotion policy that makes it difficult for women and people of color to advance in the organization. Socially conscious OD consultants also have a moral obligation to analyze and negotiate power relations in a manner that facilitates socially conscious thought and action in the organization. OD cannot be neutral with the complexity of social, political, and environmental factors involved in the practice. Rather, OD is a highly political practice where power, political institutions, social issues, and the interests of multiple parties interface. Finally, socially responsible practice promotes the use of organization resources to create social benefit and improve social welfare. This underscores the importance of the organization's use of resources and power to foster benefit to society. Socially conscious organizations actively seek ways to use their money and influence to improve society.

SUMMARY

This chapter has addressed the stakeholder aspect of the OD framework which also considers the consultant, the context, and the process of OD from a critical perspective. The chapter defined the stakeholder, taking a broad approach to considering not only the primary stakeholders in an OD intervention such as management and employees, but also the secondary stakeholders who will be affected by the actions and outcomes of the OD process. The chapter defined what is meant by the OD client, noting that it is not always immediately obvious who the client is in an OD process. The consultant must use the contracting process to identify the primary client. The chapter also introduced the concept of positionality which is not widely discussed in mainstream OD. Positionality helps us understand how the visible and invisible identities of the people involved in the OD process shape power relations and the negotiation over interests. The chapter based recommendations for negotiating stakeholder needs in a contested context shaped by positionality and power, by consulting Cervero and Wilson's model of program planning that comes from the adult education literature.

Being stakeholder-oriented is a challenge for OD consultants in a context where needs are competing and constantly being negotiated. Advocating for stakeholders and practicing corporate social responsibility put new demands on OD consultants. This requires ongoing reflective practice on your positionality and power, and careful consideration of what outcomes matter to stakeholders. It is a commitment to both personal and professional standards for ethics and integrity (see for example Academy of Human Resource Development, 1999). It also requires us to learn new frameworks and tools for understanding and implementing our work. Considering stakeholders means that we must recognize that certain interests are privileged when decisions are made. It is imperative to raise questions such as "Who benefits from the OD process?" and "Are we generating outcomes that matter?"

CHAPTER 5

The Context

Context is the social system that permeates the thinking and actions of all human beings within a particular social situation such as a classroom, school, organization, community, or nation. It is a complex intersection of positionality, the location of the social interaction, and the interests at stake. Although contexts and experiences differ, they profoundly shape our learning as described by Merriam and Caffarella (1999) in the context of adult education:

> Adult learning in context has a structural dimension which acknowledges that our society has become highly multicultural and diverse and that political and economic conditions often shape the learning experience. It is no longer a question of whether in adult learning situations we need to address issues of race, class, gender, culture, ethnicity, and sexual orientation, but rather a question of how should we deal with these issues, both in terms of who presently constitutes the majority of learners, at least in formal adult learning activities, and who should be involved. We need to know the backgrounds and experiences of our learners, as individual learners, but also as member of socially and culturally constructed groups such as women and men; poor, middle-class, and rich; and black, white, and brown. These socially constructed notions of who our learners are and we are as educators and subsequent power dynamics should be given the same attention in teaching and learning, planning, and administrative functions of the technology of our practice. (p. 196)

The awareness of context and diversity described by Merriam and Caffarella is important in OD practice, which is vitally dependent on learning. A more critical approach to OD is concerned with whether its efforts facilitate social change or replicate the status quo. Social disparities are reflected in OD practices when only certain people get training and promotions (often white males receive such OD perks disproportionately to women and people of color), or cultural change initiatives aimed at ramping up speed and service force certain workers to attend meetings at times that interfere with their home life (such initiatives usually impact women negatively who are socially expected to handle the brunt of child and elder care). Context shapes the people, process, data, intervention, and results, and deserves our attention when planning organization development (OD).

This chapter presents the context as part of the book's framework for understanding the consultant, stakeholder, context, and interventions within a critical OD perspective. Taking a more critical approach to OD necessitates critiquing the context and understanding how power relations shape it. It means understanding the unintended consequences of OD interventions and ways organization change can be more equitable. This chapter defines the features of organization context, reviews how diversity impacts OD, and offers strategies for making OD an inclusive, democratic process.

THE FEATURES OF ORGANIZATION CONTEXT

A key feature of the framework for this book is to understand the dynamic context in which OD occurs. This context incorporates the people, positionalities, power, and politics that shape and influence OD activities. Context extends beyond organization walls to include the social milieu shaped by politics and culture. Failure to appreciate and accommodate context promises trouble for any OD consultant. Unfortunately, much of OD theory and practice overlooks or underestimates the contextual influences of power dynamics, culture, and positionality. Yet, ignoring context defies OD's reverence for systems thinking, a key OD competency. Incorporating an appreciation for context into your critical OD repertoire will help you see how it influences every level of the OD process from the individual to the community. It will also help you navigate the political waters of organization change.

Context is influenced by place, positionality, and power. The confluence of these forces shapes the privilege and prestige of its inhabitants. Place (or environment) is a multifaceted physical and psychological space in which social action is situated, such as an organization. It may incorporate physical conditions, political conditions, economic conditions, power dynamics, and other influences that impact the people occupying that space. Place may also require its inhabitants to modify their thinking and action when they are occupying the space. For instance, some organizations are highly formal and lines of command are carefully followed, such as governmental organizations. Within the space of this type of organization, you might notice conservative dress and demeanor and that people do not go outside formal communication channels to accomplish their tasks. On the other hand, an organization might be highly informal such as a busy nonprofit with a small staff. The organization space is busy and casual and no one follows formal protocols for communication since the organization is so flat hierarchically. There is a psychological undercurrent of activism and commitment to the cause. Money is always tight, and the space reflects creative use of resources to make it welcoming, yet economical. Change initiatives, characteristic of OD, often require modifications of psychological and physical spaces, thus causing trepidation among those affected. Spatial changes may occur due to a change in location or even a change in leadership. When such changes occur, rules and cultural practices may change. Place is not a fixed entity as both physical and psychological spaces have people and their intersecting positionalities continually moving in and out of them, shaping and reshaping the dynamics and power relations.

Positionality was introduced in Chapter 4 and profoundly impacts interpersonal relationships and influences interactions within social context. It is important for us to recognize and counter how positionality contributes to asymmetrical power relations in the OD process. This includes not only an awareness of and ability to reflect on our own positionality, but also to see how it intersects with other positionalities and contexts. We continually enact our positionalities within relationships of power in context and in turn other people react to us as well as enact their own positionalities. Intersecting positionalities confer or disallow prestige and privilege. This creates a dynamic and complex web of positional and political intersections within context that impact the OD process. For some of us, power and prestige will be correlated with our role as consultants and experts. This is especially true if you are an external consultant. For others, gaining power and prestige in the consulting relationship may be mitigated by our positionality. We may encounter resistance because our role represents impending change, or our clients may resist us based on factors of our positionality such as gender, race, or age, regardless of how well we are trained in our areas.

Power was also defined in Chapter 4. People exercise power as they interact and negotiate for interests in the OD process. Power may be exercised by deciding who is invited to attend a planning meeting, and who is excluded. It may be used in deciding what information to share and what to conceal. It may be useful in influencing others if you have positional or expert power to persuade them to your thinking. Power has been defined as the ability to pose one's will on others, or to influence outcomes. OD consulting is often described as attempting to influence clients without formal power or authority, making an understanding of power and context of high importance to effective consulting practice. As an OD consultant, you are constantly exercising power within various contexts, although you rarely see this reality discussed in OD texts. The exercise of power happens through relationships, and as previously discussed, OD is based on trusting, open relationships between the consultant and the client. As pointed out earlier, simply your presence as an OD consultant has power and can serve as an intervention because it affects the client's interaction and thinking about the problem you've been hired to address. As OD consultants, we have an opportunity to attend to contextual issues through interventions that acknowledge and account for the dynamics of social interaction: place, positionality, and power. When designing interventions, it is important for us to understand various positionalities in their environments as Tisdell (1995) has pointed out in educational contexts. Positionality may result in an individual being marginalized or privileged, depending on the context.

We are awash in systems of power that are historically racist and sexist that are organized to protect the interests of dominant power, most often white males. Issues of less dominant groups are invisible as Merriam and Caffarella (1999) observe "not everyone wants to admit that the issues of race, ethnicity, gender, and sexual orientation have or should have any relevance" (p. 127). Social context and positionality are important issues to consider in contemporary education and in the learning process of adults because they impact adult life. Some people are oppressed by other individuals or society because of their social positions. It is, therefore, necessary to acknowledge them in organization development.

OD's espoused theory is one of inclusivity and appreciation for diversity, and most would argue that it is not a racist or sexist practice. Yet, the key question is not whether or not OD is racist or sexist, but whether it is anti-racist and anti-sexist. Although diversity is an espoused value of the field, it is not OD's theory in use. To illustrate this point, OD textbooks give issues related to power, diversity, and politics short shrift and this systematic exclusion should give the field pause. For instance, the 2006 *Organization Development Reader* has power indexed in only 10 of its 1057 pages. The discussion of power within those pages does not address issues related to positionality or the role of power in OD consulting work. Only one of the book's 47 chapters is devoted to diversity. Race does not appear in the index of this large volume. Power in this text is discussed as a power lab (Mirvis, 2006), the use of power in conflict (Parker, 2006), distribution of power (Galbraith, 2006), and power-over strategies (Merron, 2006). Classic OD textbooks by Cummings and Worley (2005) and French and Bell (1999) also do a poor job of addressing contextual issues. The situation in HRD is also problematic and "Much of the current management and training literature is sparse about how issues of gender and power inform the day-to-day experiences of HRD managers" (Hanscome & Cervero, 2003, p. 511). Hanscome and Cervero observe that what exists tends to focus on diversity practices and strategies for scaling the career ladder. They contend, "Serious discussion about the real-life connections between gender and power at the organizational level is also absent in many HRD training texts" (p. 512). They surveyed several popular HRD textbooks (Cummings & Worley, 1993; Johns, 1996; Raymond et al., 1996) and concluded:

> Women's workplace challenges were subsumed under the umbrella of organizational diversity or pay issues, thus seri-

ously diluting the everyday problems that women experience. Although gender and power appear as separate listings in the indexes, they are not connected, as in cross-referencing or sub-indexing. As well, although power is linked to hierarchal structures, gender inequalities are only briefly mentioned in terms of the glass ceiling. (p. 512)

Adding a sincere discussion of power and positionality within context to the OD discourse is sorely needed. Adult education's advances in this area offer a foundation for OD to begin considering these dynamics. The next section will address diversity as an OD issue and identify ways you can attend to contextual issues related to diversity in your practice. The landscape of the United States is shifting and underscores the need to consider context in practicing OD responsibly.

HOW DIVERSITY IMPACTS OD

To gain further appreciation for context, this section provides a brief snapshot of how changing demographics are affecting organizations and OD processes. The U.S. workforce is illustrative of how diverse, multicultural, and global the world is becoming. Organizations mimic the broader society, making them interesting case studies of sociocultural dynamics. When OD fails to acknowledge the dynamic complexity of context, it immediately compromises itself. When OD ignores race and gender and other positionalities, it reinforces systems of racism and sexism in organizations. The forces at play in context profoundly impact every process of OD and can have a major influence on the overall results of the intervention. It is important to consider these forces if OD is to be an anti-oppression intervention in organizations.

Mindfulness of context depends on the exploration of cultural dimensions and assumptions about differences in the workplace to help workers recognize cultural identity and to challenge workplace management of these identities (Fenwick, 2001). Because the workplace is the only context where workers have the opportunity to learn about and develop vocational knowledge, the need for attending to its context is becoming more and more important (Billet, 2001; Bradford, 1999), especially since most adults work for pay during their lifetime and spend up to one-third of their lives working. Although organizations play an enormous role in people's work lives, they are not equally hospitable to all members. Both organizations and workers are unique, bringing values, cultures, identities, and social norms together that coalesce into the complex sociocultural system of work, making it a rich and challenging environment for the practice of OD. It is important for us as OD consultants to be keenly aware of the dynamics of the workplace, since inequitable practices and policies often go unnoticed, they are so intertwined with the culture.

If you are not a white male in the U.S. workplace, chances are you are not benefiting equally from many OD interventions. For instance, you may have less access to training and development programs, receive fewer promotions, suppress your identity in order to assimilate to patriarchal culture, and experience harassment or other mistreatment. If English is not your first language, you are likely to be excluded from developmental programs and may be forced to suppress your cultural or religious heritage. If you are an older worker, you may be excluded from training programs and overlooked for promotional opportunities. These dynamics pose additional challenges to the practice of OD in that not all workers are treated equally.

The U.S. workforce is predicted to continue changing dramatically over the next 100 years according to the U.S. Census Bureau. The population is expected to grow slowly and age rapidly, while immigration continues to increase (Little & Triest, 2002). Data from the Immigration and Naturalization Service (INS) indicate that immigrants have supplied approximately 35% of the U.S. population growth, and about 40% growth in the labor force since the mid 1960s (Little & Triest, 2002; U.S. Immigration and Naturalization Service, 1999). The composition of immigrants to America has changed from Europeans to people of Latino and Asian descent, and it is predicted that two-thirds of new entrants into the global workforce will come from the developing countries (Graig, Haley, Luss, & Schieber, 2002). Yet, there is significant backlash against immigrants in the

U.S. context at the moment. In spite of the resistance, immigration has created new issues for organizations to address: language and religion.

Aging workers, women, people of color, gays and lesbians, immigrants, and religious groups populate today's workplace posing challenges in creating workplaces and OD processes that are inclusive. It has been found that these groups are often marginalized when it comes to receiving OD interventions such as training and development when compared to white males (Bierema, 2002; Thomas, 2005). Many OD interventions involve activities that bring diverse groups together. Some of these include communication, training, developmental relationships (e.g., mentoring, sponsorship, coaching), performance feedback, survey feedback, teambuilding, and strategic planning, to name a few. As a critical OD consultant, you are not only examining how organization structure and policy affect stakeholders, but also how such factors might negatively impact groups that have a history of marginalization in the organization.

Several years ago I worked in a manufacturing setting in a rural setting in the southeast. After some time in the plant, I noticed that only women worked in the lowest-paid assembly jobs. All of the men worked in the semi- and skilled-trades jobs, with the exception of one woman in a 200-person plant. There were unspoken cultural rules and policies that segregated the jobs by gender. I began working to correct this imbalance, but faced an uphill culture battle when encouraging employees to consider non-traditional jobs. Women resisted being promoted to the semi and skilled trades, even though the pay was better, viewing these jobs as "men's work." At one time we also had a low performing male skilled trade worker. He quit before he would allow himself to be "demoted" to "women's work." I had my work cut out for me attempting to break this hegemonic cycle that perpetuated gender segregation in the workplace and persistent poverty in the community. Yet, an understanding of power and positionality was helpful in diagnosing that the problem was structural and cultural. Addressing it was a long-range intervention that also required working with management and the human resources personnel on issues related to recruitment, orientation, training, and performance feedback. Our well-functioning recruitment and retentions programs were not working at all to address the inequities inherent in the workplace, even though they appeared to be working well if the only variables being considered were keeping jobs filled and running the plant to full capacity.

One of the issues in the manufacturing example above was a lack of access to training. The culture of job segregation dictated that management didn't push the women into non-traditional roles and the women wanted nothing to do with them. Although this example was quite extreme, it is common for developmental opportunity to be unequally distributed in organizations. Not all workers receive the same level or amount of development. Women have historically lacked access to the same type of development men enjoy or exposure to jobs and experiences that make them promotable. The U.S. Department of Labor reports that 55-64 year olds were only one third as likely to receive training as 35-44 year olds, and older workers attending training were often mistreated and viewed as "untrainable" (Maurer & Rafuse, 2001).

This brief synopsis of the employment and developmental status of marginalized groups in the U.S. workforce is a solemn reminder that not all OD interventions are created equally or distributed fairly. Consideration of context in OD means committing to making it as inclusive and democratic as possible and being aware of how various positionalities are at a disadvantage in organizations.

THE CASE OF WOMEN IN THE UNITED STATES

The previous section identified some developmental issues faced by marginalized groups in the U.S. work context. This section will examine women workers in more depth to show how context impacts their ability to succeed in organizations. Often this exclusion is tied to OD activities. A critical OD scrutinizes organization practices and pays attention to who gets trained, promoted, and developed to help create more equity.

Women have historically been segregated into gendered work and relegated into low-paying jobs that have little potential for advancement. Women's employment status in feminized occupations is a persistent trend that is resulting in less opportunity and a sustained wage gap.

The International Labor Organization (ILO) reported in 1990 that women were excluded from high-profile training programs 38.8% of the time, yet over 39% of employers felt the trend was an a non-issue. In a report on Global Employment Trends for Women, the ILO (2007) concluded, "More women then ever before are in work, but a persistent gap in status, job security, wages and education between women and men is contributing to the 'feminization of working poverty.'"

Education and training are a key component to help women progress, along with creating policies, structures, and cultures in organizations that promote their advancement. Women and men receive different developmental experiences in their careers (Federal Glass Ceiling Commission, 1998; Knoke & Isho, 1998; Ohlott, Ruderman, & McCauley, 1994). In fact, Still (1985) found that men tend to be sent to promotion-oriented training whereas women receive maintenance-oriented training that is geared toward developing functional skills for their current jobs. This trend continues today with women receiving fewer line assignments that lead to advancement than men. Male-dominated managerial hierarchies decrease women's opportunities for career encouragement and training (Tharenou, Latimer, & Conroy, 1994) and women do not have equal access to management development programs (Limerick & Heywood, 1993; Still, 1985). Just as in management, women tend to become sidelined and marginalized in management education and experiences that would groom them for ascending the career ladder. Women are also at a developmental disadvantage in the workplace because of the hidden curriculum that teaches them how to assimilate patriarchal culture and the expectations that they will suppress their female identity in order to succeed by masculine standards (Bierema, 2001; Hayes & Flannery, 2000). Social expectations for the "ideal worker" are gendered and businesses define them through masculine criteria such as aggressiveness, independence, devotion, non-emotionality, and rationality (Rothausen-Vange, 2004).

The 2006 Census of Women Corporate Officers, Top Earners, and Directors of the Fortune 500 (Catalyst, 2007) showed a persistent shortage of women in leadership roles and concluded that at the current rate of change it would take 47 years for women to reach parity with men in the *Fortune 500*. Although women number 50% of current managerial and professional occupations, they hold only 14.6% of the top positions. During 2006, the number of corporate officers decreased from 2005 and women were still more likely to populate staff positions. Line positions tend to lead to higher advancement, yet women are still being channeled to more gender-appropriate roles. Top women earners increased 0.3% in 2006. The case of board directors is even grimmer, also decreasing in 2006. It is projected that it will take women 73 years to reach parity with men as board directors. The lack of substantive advancement of women in organizations across the decades is a persistent problem that could be addressed by OD in a number of ways including recruitment and retention, developmental relationships, feedback and rewards systems, culture change, and action learning.

Neither women nor people of color enjoy proportionate representation at executive levels in organizations, considering their sheer numbers in the workplace. Citing Kanter's (1997) notion of homosocial reproduction systems, or the ways in which both women and men sustain gender roles and restrictions, Thomas (2005) suggests this imbalance of women and people of color's recruitment, retention, and advancement reflects "male managers' need to reproduce themselves in order to reduce the uncertainty that is naturally occurring in managerial jobs" (pp. 19-20). This reproduction of dominant power is called consensual validation and is expressed through a desire to recruit and promote others who fit with one's own values, beliefs, and attitudes. The benefit of this phenomenon is that:

> By surrounding themselves with others who are like them and who are likely to conform to the status quo, these managers limit the extent to which their ideas, beliefs and attitudes are challenged by dissimilar others—instead they are affirmed and validated. (p. 20)

This phenomenon was also at play in the previous manufacturing example where the jobs were segregated by gender. Greenhaus, Parasuraman, and Wormley (1990) examined relationships among race, organizational experiences, job performance evaluations, and career outcomes for black and white managers from three organizations. They found that, compared to white managers, blacks felt less accepted, viewed themselves as having less job discretion, received lower performance ratings, were more likely to have reached career plateaus, and experienced less career satisfaction.

In another study, Catalyst (2007) examined gender stereotyping at work, identifying it as a key barrier to advancement. Gender stereotyping causes women's talents to be routinely underestimated and underutilized. The OD solution is not changing women's leadership styles. It is about fundamentally addressing gender stereotyping. Changes of this magnitude are extremely difficult to address because they involve changing deeply held opinions and assumptions about women. Catalyst found that men and women actually exhibit similar leadership styles, but that women are so subjected to gender stereotypes that they are in a "double bind" or "no win" situation. Men are still viewed as default leaders and women as atypical ones. Some of the stereotypes include extreme perceptions of women leaders (they are either too "soft" or too "tough"). Women also face tougher standards than men, yet receive lower rewards. The old adage about "working twice as hard for half the pay" holds true according to the Catalyst study. Finally, competent women who adopt a more masculine style tend to be disliked more than those adopting a more gendered feminine style. Catalyst advocates significant change to rid organizations of such damaging stereotypes that will require shifting culture norms. Learning about stereotypes is the first step. They also recommend providing women leaders and other employees with the support and resources necessary to increase awareness of women's leadership skills and the damaging effects of stereotypes. They also advocate creating innovative work practices that target stereotypic bias such as diversity education and performance evaluations that reward behaviors that challenge gender stereotyping. All of Catalyst's suggestions are OD interventions.

Several authors have noted that although extensive research exists considering variables that hinder women's advancement, scarce literature exists about factors that facilitate such development (Hite & McDonald, 2004; Knorr, 2005; Osipow & Fitzgerald, 1996).

Hite and McDonald also point out that the majority of research on women's careers focuses on college-educated managers, not non-managerial women. They conducted focus groups with 26 non-managerial women and found their participants adapted their career goals to meet other life circumstances; and that family responsibilities, job security, and organizational support systems influence their career success and satisfaction.

Hite (2004) surveyed black and white women managers and found differences in their perceptions of opportunities available based on race and gender. Black and white women share similar views when comparing opportunities between white women and men for getting hired, being promoted, receiving salary increases, and facing other workplace challenges. When making comparisons with either men or women of color, white women were far more optimistic about the opportunities for people of color than were black women. Hite's study explores how issues of race are ignored among whites and OD practitioners.

Developing women in organizations and targeting OD practices to correct disparities are not just good OD practice, but also can be profitable. Catalyst (2008) reports a direct correlation between how well a company performs and the percentage of women executives it employs. According to the report, conducted by Catalyst, "Advancing Women Leaders: The Connection Between Women Board Directors and Women Corporate Officers," companies with the largest percentage of female board directors and corporate officers achieve higher financial performances as a whole. Catalyst also drew a connection between the future number of women in senior management and the present number of women on a corporate board. According to researchers, companies with boards made up of 30% of women in 2001 had an average of 45% more female corporate officers by 2006, versus companies without female board members.

This examination of women's workplace status underscores that OD has significant potential to impact the development of marginalized workers in organizations. It is not just a matter of ensuring developmental opportunities are made available, but also to ensure that they are equitable with the quantity and quality of men's development.

MAKING OD INCLUSIVE, DEMOCRATIC, AND EMANCIPATORY

This book has made the case that OD tends to be performative and managerialist, overlooks positionality, and consequently may not be democratic. The previous examination of women's plight in U.S. organizations underscores these challenges. The Catalyst research has made some excellent suggestions for addressing inequity in organizations, many of the suggestions being OD interventions. Often OD efforts focus on enhancing organization and managerial interests such as improving productivity, performance, and profitability, but not necessarily on considering employee needs and interests or overall organization health when making such changes. Organization development is often performance based, managerial driven, and sometimes damaging to an adult's sense of identity, self-worth, and control because it attempts to be culturally neutral. Striving to make OD more inclusive and democratic is one measure we can take to offset the performative bias of organization change and development efforts and create more balanced OD interventions and outcomes.

There are several steps we can take to be context-sensitive and honor the diverse identities and positionalities in organizations. These include critically analyzing the culture; seeking a democratic OD process; incorporating diversity; creating inclusive OD practices; and making OD emancipatory.

Analyzing the Culture

Organization culture is a common target of OD interventions as seen in the Catalyst examples. Changing it, however, is extremely difficult and requires a long-term commitment. Even if the culture is not the aim of the OD intervention, it significantly impacts any type of intervention and must be accurately understood if OD efforts are to be effective. By critically analyzing culture we can identify cultural forces that drive organization norms, practices, and policies.

Culture has been defined as the collective programming of the mind, which distinguishes the members of one group from another (Hofstede, 1986). Culture has also been described as an integrated system of learned behavior patterns that are characteristic of the members of any given society. Culture refers to the total way of life of a particular group of people. It includes everything that a group of people thinks, says, does, and makes—its customs, language, material artifacts, and shared systems of attitudes and feelings. Schein (1990) defined it as:

- Culture is a pattern of basic assumptions.
- The assumptions are invented, discovered, or developed by a given group.
- Assumptions are made as the group learns to cope with its problems of external adaptations and internal integration.
- Culture is to be taught to new members.
- Culture delineates the correct ways to perceive, think, and feel in relations to problems of external adaptation and internal integration.

Based on these definitions, it is apparent how powerful culture can be at maintaining the status quo since so many features of culture make it a deeply ingrained process that new members must learn and emulate if they wish to be accepted in the culture. Culture is tacit knowledge making it resilient to change since it is built upon mental models and behaviors that become taken for granted over time, even when the practices of a culture perpetuate inequities.

Often, OD initiatives strive to change organization culture. Changing the culture is a complex process that requires utmost commitment from leaders. Changing the culture is not a matter of issuing edicts such as "we are going to change the culture to being more sustainable . . . or equitable . . . or quality focused." Rather, it is a complicated process of challenging and changing deeply held assumptions or mental models about functioning within the organization. Women's integration into the workplace remains a challenging example of culture change. Although women make up 50% of the U.S. workplace, they are still viewed as unequal and not paid or promoted on par with men (ILO, 2004). We live in a culture that still expects clear demarcations between women's and men's work and they are difficult to change. Simply declaring "we value women here" is of little meaning, as is ordering management to suddenly behave differently.

CULTURE Vs.
CLIMATE
(P. 110)

t to understand and con- o "take the pulse" of the rienced and perceived at s of what is happening in . These feelings are more :cted within much shorter s, or weeks. Organization s to the environment that d peers, formally and in- by how their leaders act ore. OD efforts aimed at er to accomplish. For ex- ;ain, it might be observed icult for women who are h as early morning meet- bout not scheduling meet- ings at the crack of dawn and there is an immediate sense that the situation has improved. That is not to say that the deeply seated patriarchal culture has changed, but that particular climate issue has.

As OD consultants, it is helpful to understand the culture and analyze it, particularly to understand power relations, policies, unspoken rules, and history. This will be easier for internal consultants since they are already a member of the culture. This can be more challenging for external consultants. The more cultural understanding you can develop, the easier it will be to work through the action research model and complete the OD process.

Tools exist for the assessment of culture (Schein, 2006), although being a savvy observer of it is also instructive. Culture surveys can provide information, but Schein argues that they cannot measure culture and that they are of little use since it is nearly impossible to know what to ask. Judging a culture survey is also problematic as the reliability and validity of the responses are difficult to assess. Schein also argues that individuals may not share the same understanding of organization phenomenon, or have issues with cultural factors that are unchangeable meaning that the survey may address a range of issues that cannot be addressed. Instead, he suggests that culture assessment is possible through a more qualitative process incorporating individual and group interviews. Assessing culture needs to be done with linkage to an organization problem or issue, such as gender stereotyping. Schein suggests this approach since it is too broad to try and assess the general culture as a whole. Assessments should attempt to identify cultural assumptions and assess them according to how they facilitate or impinge meeting desired goals. For example, we might study how gender stereotyping impacts retention of women. He also reminds us to be aware of cultural subgroups and to be particularly mindful of how culture is manifest through artifacts. Schein offers an exercise to decipher organization culture. He recommends having a facilitator and following these steps:

1. Define the "business problem." This means identifying a specific problem or issue to use as you consider the culture of the organization.
2. Review the concept of culture. This includes understanding culture as visible artifacts, espoused values, and shared tacit assumptions.
3. Identify artifacts. This involves identifying artifacts that characterize your organization.
4. Identify your organization's values. This is a list of espoused values or stated beliefs about what the organization values. These may be part of the formal vision statements, but don't necessarily have to be.
5. Compare values with artifacts. This check allows us to see how consistent the espoused values are with reality.
6. Repeat the process with other groups.
7. Assess the shared assumptions. This is particularly important since culture is so difficult to change. Assumptions can give you real insight into what needs to occur.

Understanding culture is paramount to effective OD. It requires us to function like anthropologists to develop a deep understanding of the culture.

Seeking a Democratic OD Process

Workplace development opportunities are not created equally. Women, people of color, gays and lesbians, older workers, and non-English speakers have less access to developmental opportunities that lead to higher pay and promotion forcing them to forge an identity in a white, male-dominated, Eurocentric world that values youth and heterosexuality. Organizations need to recognize these inequities and provide training and development that provides more equal access to higher pay and promotion for diverse organization stakeholders. To this end, we have a responsibility to take inventory of the demographic makeup of participants in educational programs and to address non-represented groups with management. For instance, non-English speakers are particularly disadvantaged because they are excluded from training or have limited ability to understand it. It is worth it to organizations to hire supervisors who speak the language of non-English speaking workers, offer English classes and incentives for learning English, and also offer non-English language classes and incentives for learning other languages to English speaking employees. This bridges understanding across the organization.

It is important to assume that OD practice is oppressive to certain groups and consciously work to ensure that such inequities are addressed in the OD process. Chapter 4 addressed stakeholders. It is important to be mindful of both primary and secondary stakeholders, and also to tune it to stakeholders whose needs are of particular consequence. Sometimes OD interventions will only concern immediate stakeholders such as shareholders and employees. It is important to ensure that the interests of each are balanced. At other times, it will be more important to consider the needs of a broader constituency of stakeholders and advocate on their behalf.

Incorporating Diversity

The American Society for Training and Development's 2002 State of the Industry Report ranked diversity as the second most prevalent concern of HRD professionals (VanBuren & Erskine, 2002), yet diversity training may falsely raise expectations, reinforce stereotypes, and create resentment among the employees it is designed to help. Thomas (2007) also argues that there is significant resistance to diversity, making it even more difficult to address these issues in organizations.

Cox (1993) defines a cultural group as one who has "an affiliation of people who collectively share certain norms, values, or traditions that are different from those of other groups" (p. 5). Cultural diversity is "the representation, in one social system, of people with distinctly different group affiliations of cultural significance"(Cox, 1993, p. 6). The dominant diversity discourse heralds pluralism and multiculturalism, and it is generally believed that celebrating diversity is universally good. Yet, Malik (2001) argues that the problem with embracing diversity and multiculturalism is that it celebrates *difference*. He notes that "the idea of difference has always been at the heart, not of the antiracist, but of the racist agenda; and the creation of a 'multiculturalist' society has been at the expense of a more equal one" (p. 32). He explains further: "The promotion of multiculturalism is a tacit admission that the barriers that separate Blacks and Whites cannot be breached and that equality has been abandoned as a social policy goal. . . . America is not multicultural; it is simply unequal" (p. 33). Campaigning for equality involves challenging accepted practices and policies, going against the grain, and seeking social transformation (Malik, 2001). Merely celebrating diversity, on the other hand, "allows us to accept society as it is—all it says is 'we live in a diverse world, enjoy it,' allowing us to accept the divisions and inequalities that characterize the world today" (Malik, 2001, p. 34). Malik (2001) concludes that only in an equal society does difference have any meaning, since only in equal societies can difference be freely chosen.

Being an advocate for diversity means being willing to see policies and practices as oppressive, even if the prevailing belief is that they are neutral and have no malintent. Although workers are different, developmental programs that overemphasize difference may fail to addresses ways of promoting equality among employees. A better approach would be to "understand an organization as a rich and complex world of relationships rather than as a set of positions" (McDaniel & Walls, 1997, p. 366). Relationships among a diverse workforce are more complex than among homogenous groups. Diverse organizations succeed at sociocultural issues when their managers and educators embrace heterogeneity; involve workers in decisions at all levels; acknowledge and work with (rather than oversimplify) the complexity of the systems; and communicate richly, multidirectionally, and candidly.

Creating Inclusive OD Practices

There is an increasing body of multicultural adult education literature. Within the context frame, it is important to acknowledge that OD decisions are political and that decisions made throughout the process are driven by the primary stakeholders' philosophical outlook, values, and positionality. Tisdell (1995) advocates the consideration of micro and macro level variables when creating inclusive environments. In OD this would incorporate consideration of the particular organization, relationships, the impacted community, society at large, and the relationship of these contexts to one another. To achieve inclusive environments it is helpful to consider what "inclusive" means and carefully assess the steps of the OD process to evaluate them for inclusivity. OD steps of data collection, analysis, intervention selection, and implementation can be evaluated to assess how implicitly or explicitly they contribute to maintaining existing power relations based on class, gender, and race. Finally it is important to reflect on how your own unconscious behavior as a consultant contributes to challenging or reproducing society's unequal power relations.

I have modified Tisdell's strategies for creating inclusive learning environments to address how OD can be an inclusive process, sensitive to power relations:

1.   Integrate affective and experiential knowledge with theoretical concepts.
2.   Pay attention to the power relations inherent in the OD process.
3.   Be aware that clients and stakeholders are positioned differently in relationship to each other.
4.   Acknowledge the power disparity between the various stakeholders (client/consultant/management/workers/affected stakeholders).

5. Identify all stakeholders and their positionality in the OD process.
6. Consider the levels of inclusivity and the levels of contexts involved in the OD process.
7. Consider how OD interventions implicitly or explicitly contribute to challenging structured power relations.
8. Adopt anti-oppression strategies.
9. Be conscious of the ways in which unconscious behavior contributes to challenging or reproducing unequal power relations.
10. Build a community based on both openness and intellectual rigor to create a democratic process.

Attending to context in OD is imperative in increasingly diverse and global settings. Our OD practice will benefit if we consider the dynamics of place, positionality, and power when creating learning experiences and rely on a pedagogy that promotes inclusion and sensitivity to diversity.

Building on the advocacy of emancipatory leadership by Corson (2000) and Thomas (2005) as a framework for addressing diversity, I propose that context-sensitive OD is emancipatory OD, seeking anti-oppression through its efforts. The attributes of emancipatory leadership include that emancipatory leaders recognize when they are beyond their depth in dealing with complex sociocultural dynamics and seek assistance. They recognize when to expand the stakeholders involved in the decision process to include others who might have interests at stake. Emancipatory leaders minimize their presence in the decision making and function by democratic, consensus-building decision making processes. They also agree to put the implementation responsibility into the hands of those identified to handle it.

SUMMARY

This chapter examined the context of OD, identifying its features as a complex web of place, positionality, and power. The chapter illustrated the impact of positionality by reviewing demographic data on groups in the workplace, contending that even well-intentioned OD practices can have oppressive consequences. Women's status in the United States was considered as an example of how contexts impact an entire demographic group. Some possible OD interventions to address women's advancement were proposed.

Often, OD programs function to advance white men in the organization and prevent less privileged groups from moving into coveted positions of power. Although this reality may not be intended, it is a consequence of organization culture, structure, policy and social history. This book has raised the issue of performative discourse (Bierema, 2000) dominating OD, which may be one reason that it overlooks development that does not fit within the masculine, productivity-oriented paradigm. As an OD consultant, you will want to be mindful of how sexist, racist, and performative biases impact organization stakeholders, and note how OD programs are designed and distributed to evaluate whether they are privileging some groups while ignoring others. A more holistic approach that considers multiple, global stakeholders will be helpful in correcting inequity and practicing critical OD.

CHAPTER 6

Critical Interventions

This book has presented a framework for understanding consulting according to the consultant, stakeholders, and context. The focus of this chapter is on the fourth aspect of the framework, the intervention. The Critical Action Research Model strives to collect and analyze data that helps diagnose organizational problems so that interventions can be identified that will address the problems with efficacy. "OD interventions are *sets of structured activities* in which selected organizational units (target groups or individuals) engage in a task or a sequence of tasks with the goals of organizational improvement and individual development" (French & Bell, 1999, p. 145). This chapter defines interventions, outlines the criteria for selecting effective interventions, identifies various types of traditional OD interventions, and profiles critical interventions.

DEFINING AN INTERVENTION

Making an intervention marks the point where a change to the system has been made. Interventions can happen at any time during the action research cycle.

> The OD practitioner, a professional versed in the theory and practice of OD, brings four sets of attributes to the organizational setting: a set of values; a set of assumptions about people, organizations, and interpersonal relationships; a set of goals for the practitioner and the organization and its members; and a set of structured activities that are the *means* for achieving the values, assumptions, and goals. These activities are what we mean by the word *interventions*. (French & Bell, 1999, pp. 145-146)

"To intervene is to enter into an ongoing system of relation-ship, to come between or among persons, groups or objects for the purpose of helping them" (Argyris, 2000, p. 117). French and Bell recognize intervention as "a set of sequenced planned actions or events intended to help an organization increase its effectiveness" (p. 143). They also suggest that interventions purposely disrupt the status quo toward a more effective state of affairs. Argyris (1970) also emphasizes that the system exists independent of the intervener and that the client-system is an "ongoing, self-responsible unity that has the obligation to be in control over its own destiny" (p. 117). Your goal as a consultant is to ultimately help the client develop action research skills so that the need for your services becomes diminished or no longer needed. Good consultants work themselves out of a job.

CRITERIA FOR MAKING AN INTERVENTION

Argyris (1970, 2000) suggests that three "primary interven-tion tasks" or conditions that must exist before making any type of intervention. First, any recommended interventions must be based on valid information. This means that the data are collected in a reputable and responsible fashion. Second, the client must maintain discretion and autonomy and only engage in an intervention based on free, informed choice. Third, the client must have an ongoing commitment to learning and change, essentially having what Argyris calls internal commitment to the change. For example, a nonprofit organization worked with a consultant to identify opportunities for growth in its services and fundraising. The consultant conducted a valid needs analysis with various stakeholder groups to provide recommendations. The data were credible to the nonprofit organi-zation based on the range of stakeholders interviewed in the pro-cess. Since the nonprofit sought the feedback and selected which interventions to work on, they had free and informed choice. Fi-nally, there was a strong commitment among the staff and board to expand. The nonprofit incorporated most of the consultant's sug-gestions and experienced the growth it was seeking.

Cummings and Worley (2005) define three major criteria for an effective intervention that focus more on organization fit and competence building than Argyris's previous list: (1) the extent to which it fits organizational needs, (2) the degree to which it is based on causal knowledge of the outcomes, and (3) the extent to which it transfers competence to the organization to manage future changes. French and Bell (1999) suggest that all interventions should have a strategy that addresses the intervention's goals, activities, and timing, and anticipates the organization's readiness to change, potential barriers, and sources of support and leadership. They recommend the following points to ensure a smooth intervention:

1.   Include the relevant stakeholders.
2.   Base the intervention on the data generated.
3.   Involve the stakeholders in the action research process.
4.   Keep the intervention focus on the key goal.
5.   Set manageable, attainable goals.
6.   Design the intervention so that key learning can be attained and shared.
7.   Emphasize collaborative learning throughout the process.
8.   Use the opportunity for the client group to enhance learning about the interpersonal workings of the group.

Cummings and Worley (1995) suggest that designing effective interventions requires attention to contingencies related to the change situation as well as to the target of change. Contingencies related to the **change situation** include the client's readiness for change, capability to change, cultural context, and the capabilities of the change agent. The case of the nonprofit and its needs analysis represents an organization that was highly ready for change. Contingencies related to the **target of change** include organizational issues such as strategy, technology and structure, human resources, and human processes. The nonprofit was less equipped to deal with these contingencies due to budget restrictions, a short-term strategic plan, insufficient technology, and a small staff. Implementing the desired changes took longer than desired until the contingencies related to the target of change could be addressed.

TYPES OF INTERVENTIONS

Even though we often have little or no formal power as consultants, our presence is an intervention that can affect the entire action research process. The list of possible interventions we can make is vast. French and Bell (1999) classify OD interventions into 14 types including:

1. Diagnostic activities.
2. Team building activities.
3. Intergroup activities.
4. Survey feedback.
5. Education and training.
6. Technostructural or structural activities.
7. Process consultation.
8. Grid-organization development.
9. Third-party peacemaking activities.
10. Coaching and counseling activities.
11. Life and career planning activities.
12. Planning and goal setting activities.
13. Strategic management activities.
14. Organizational transformation activities.

They also offer a classification of OD activities according to the target of the intervention. They classify these according to individuals, dyads or triads, teams and groups, intergroup relations, and the total organization. Cummings and Worley (2005) organize interventions according to human process interventions, techno structural interventions, human resource management interventions, and strategic change interventions.

No matter how you classify interventions, each part of the OD process builds toward making one. Interventions may occur at any point in the action research cycle and are implemented to address the issue or problem at hand. The most effective interventions are valid and relevant to the stakeholders and can be either diagnostic (occurring during the discovery or data collection phase) or confrontive (based on data analysis). Interventions can also be classified according to the unit of analysis such as individual, group, organizational, and sociotechnical. OD interventions may span levels (for instance, a performance management system intervention will affect both individuals and the organization) and have multiple purposes (individual development and organization streamlining).

Table 6.1 Levels of Traditional OD Interventions

Individual Level Interventions	Group Level Interventions	Organization Level Interventions	Sociotechnical Interventions
• T-groups • Training and development • Leadership and management development • Performance management • 360 degree feedback • Developmental relationships • Coaching • Career and life planning • Self-awareness tools (e.g., MBTI) • Reflective practice • Action learning	• Process counsulting • Teambuilding • Team learning • Diversity interventions • Virtual teams • Conflict management • Third-party intervention • Dialogue • Appreciative inquiry • Action science • Total quality management • Quality of worklife programs	• Vision, values, mission development • Strategic planning • Survey feedback • Confrontation meetings • Grid OD • Large-scale OD	• Organization design • Reorganization • Work redesign

Examples of interventions according to level of analysis are outlined in Table 6.1. It is beyond the scope of this book to present an exhaustive listing and complete description of every OD intervention. Extensive discussion of OD interventions can be found in Cummings (2007), McLean, (2006), Cummings and Worley (2005), French and Bell (1999), French, Bell, and Zawacki (2000).

Schein (1988) identifies two types of interventions, diagnostic and confrontive. **Diagnostic interventions** occur in the process of collecting data and can happen at any time during the OD process. Even your mere presence is an intervention to the client as you represent action on a problem and possible change. "Every decision to observe something, to ask a question, or to meet with someone constitutes an intervention into the ongoing organizational process" (Schein, 1988, p. 141). Schein belabors this point suggesting that research models "make the glib assumption that one gathers data *prior* to intervening" (p. 142). He further emphasizes,

The correct assumption is that every act on the part of the process consultant—event the initial act of deciding to work with the organization—constitutes an intervention. . . . The main implication of this latter assumption is that the consultant must think through everything he does in terms of its probable impact on the organization. (p. 142)

The other type of intervention is confrontive. **Confrontive interventions** are based on data that were generated as a result of the data collection process. Schein (1988) has offered a classification of confrontive interventions, although he cautions that they should not be rigidly classified:

A.   Agenda-managed interventions.
    a. Questions that direct attention to process issues.
    b. Process-analysis periods.
    c. Meetings devoted to process issues.
    d. Conceptual inputs on process-related topics.
B.   Feedback of observations or other data.
    a. Feedback to groups during process analysis or regular work time.
    b. Feedback to individuals after meetings or after data gathering.
C.   Coaching or counseling of individuals or groups.
D.   Structural suggestions.
    a. Pertaining to group membership.
    b. Pertaining to communication or interaction patterns.
    c. Pertaining to allocation of work, assignment of responsibility, and lines of authority (pp. 148-149).

Schein (1988) notes that the preceding outline is organized according to descending likelihood of the intervention's use. He suggests that he is most often likely to make an intervention that relates to the group's agenda and least likely to recommend structural changes. Schein suggests that management problems (e.g., sales marketing or production) do not qualify for process consulting because they put the consultant into the role of an expert resource instead of a process consultant. The next sections will briefly summarize Schein's categories of interventions.

Agenda-Managed Interventions

Schein acknowledges that helping a group manage its agenda may seem like a weak intervention, yet emphasizes that the overarching purpose of agenda management is to help sensitize the group to its own internal processes. He suggests that something as simple as evaluating meetings turns group members' attention to how they felt during the meeting and how they reacted to communication or how decisions were made. Schein notes, "the more interested the group becomes in its own workings, the more time it devotes to discussing this topic and the less time there is for its regular agenda" (p. 150). He cautions that the consultant should not move too quickly to analysis of process issues in the group such as "relationships" or "interpersonal issues." Members must be emotionally ready and willing to deal with the risks and feelings that will emerge when addressing such issues. Often groups arrive at an impasse about what issues they should be focusing on and agenda management interventions help to influence the groups' process. Schein regards agenda management as a confrontive intervention because it underscores issues that the client cannot evade in the presence of other colleagues.

Confronting through the Use of Feedback

The next level of confrontive intervention, confronting through the use of feedback, is the feedback of observation or other data to groups. This is a step of the action research model and most OD incorporates some type of feedback. Schein recommends this type of intervention when the group has agreed to examine interpersonal processes and invited the consultant to survey individual group members for their reactions and feelings. Another time this type of intervention is appropriate is where the group is already competent at and comfortable with discussions of interpersonal process and wishes to supplement the discussion with more personal feedback. Confronting through feedback requires that group members exhibit readiness for feedback and agreement that engaging in such a process would be a legitimate activity for the group. Schein cautions

that the consultant must exercise restraint in sharing personal observations; the role is to help the individuals or groups use the data
themselves. Schein (1988) emphasizes, "The issue is not whether
the observation is valid. The issue is whether the group is able and
ready to understand and learn from the observation. Such ability
and readiness must be built up before the feedback can be useful"
(p. 160). The goal is to help the group develop skills of providing
feedback and input and to rely less and less on the consultant for
such feedback.

For this type of feedback to be effective, it often works best to
share the feedback with individuals first and next the group. The
consultant's job is to make sure that participants understand and
accept the feedback so appropriate action can take place. Individual
feedback is warranted when data have been gathered on the individual via observation or interview, and the individual exhibits readiness to hear the feedback (Schein, 1988).

Observation listening and the ability to ask the right questions
facilitate learning, diffuse defensiveness, and engender tact and di-
plomacy when delivering threatening information. You must also
be willing to hear feedback on your own performance. Your reac-
tion will serve as a model for other individuals and groups involved
in the intervention. The clients' ability to give feedback also is a
signal to the consultant of how well they are learning to function
without the consultant.

Coaching and Counseling

Although coaching is a large trend among consultants, Schein
advises that it should be used relatively rarely in comparison to less
threatening interventions already discussed. Coaching and counseling interventions are more powerful and thus require more caution and care on the part of the consultant.

Upon receiving feedback, Schein (1988) notes that it is typical for both individuals and groups to ask for help in modifying
their behavior to get the desired results. He emphasizes that consultants should not answer such questions until they are sure that the
individuals or groups have understood the feedback and related it

to concrete, observable behavior, and they have begun to try and solve the problem themselves.

> It is essential to help the client improve his ability to observe and process data about himself, to help him accept and learn from feedback, and to help him become an active participant with the counselor/consultant in identifying and solving his own problems. (Schein, 1988, pp. 168-169)

Schein suggests that the major difference between being a counselor and a consultant is that the consultant usually has more data on the individual or group's behavior.

Structural Interventions

Schein (1988) suggests that recommending structural innovations is relatively rare in process consulting since consultants are not usually equipped to make recommendations for allocation of work, modification of communications, or organization of committees. Schein emphasizes that our job is not to make suggestions, but rather to help the client generate solutions. The exception to this rule is when the client wants to design a process to work on organizational or interpersonal problems, or wishes to design a data collection process to address a problem. When we possess relevant expertise and experience, then we have an obligation to share that knowledge with the client. Schein (1988) advocates that we should not withhold our expertise from the client but not confuse being an expert with helping the organization learn how to solve its own problems.

The intervention consists of moving the client from the current state through a transitional phase and into the new, desired state. Most change requires learning. Learning is necessary in becoming aware of a problem or opportunity that propels individuals, groups, or organizations toward a change. Learning is imperative as the clients grapple with how to move through the transitional phase where they are essentially letting go of old learning, gaining new knowledge, and creating supports to maintain the new learning. Finally, once the desired state is achieved, learning must continue to maintain and improve upon the change.

MAKING CRITICAL INTERVENTIONS

This book has focused on taking a more mindful, critical approach to OD with a particular focus on adult educators and HRD practitioners. Traditional OD is often presented as a neutral, rational approach to solving organization problems. Yet, you know from your own organization that every intervention impacts power relations, interpersonal communications, job opportunities, and the environment. Interventions are not neutral. The previous sections have articulated practical considerations for making interventions as well as described various types of interventions. Most OD interventions can be implemented with a critical orientation, depending on the consultant, but what makes an intervention critical?

1.   It is practiced by a critical OD consultant.
2.   It is concerned with enhancing organization well-being.
3.   It disrupts the status quo and prevailing power relations.
4.   It creates more democratic, equitable practices, policies, and structures.

Building a critical OD consultancy is the goal of this book. It is based on the vision of committed consultants who engage in OD work with a sense of stewardship and commitment to creating changes that promote organization well-being.

The previous section showed ways of classifying OD interventions according to unit of analysis (individual, team, organization, and sociotechnical) or category of intervention (agenda-managed interventions, feedback, coaching and counseling, and structural suggestions). A critical intervention could fall into any of these categories. Additionally, there are certain interventions that can advance organizational well-being and critical OD if used either individually or in conjunction with traditional OD interventions.

This section presents critical interventions organized into five areas: (1) conversational interventions that help us use talk to ad-

Table 6.2 Critical OD Interventions

Conversational Interventions	Opportunistic Interventions
• Dialogue	• Small wins
• Fierce conversations	• Variable-term opportunism
• Verbal jujitsu	
Learning Interventions	Coalition Building Interventions
• Reflective practice	• Networks
• Critical action technologies	• Strategic alliance building
Activism Interventions	
• Disruptive self-expression	
• Tempered radicalism	

vance a change agenda; (2) opportunistic interventions that take advantage of unexpected or unanticipated opportunities to make change; (3) learning interventions to leverage educational opportunities to ensure lasting and effective change, building on our unique expertise in adult learning; (4) coalition building interventions that emphasize how to rely on strategic relationships with other individuals or groups to advance change agendas; and (5) activism interventions, or those acts that directly challenge the status quo. These critical interventions build on skills that are usually a part of our repertoire as adult educators and HRD professions and are summarized in Table 6.2.

Conversational Interventions

In your work, you are responsible for bringing groups together whether for team meetings, problem solving, or strategic planning. So much of our work in organizations relies on having conversations. Yet, not all conversations are created equally, and not every person is a good conversationalist. Being effective at conversations means that you bring a sense of inquiry and willingness to reflect to the table. Although it may seem obvious, being an effective conversant and helping others build those skills are important ways you can impact your organization. Conversational interventions use communication as a tool for creating change through careful attention to the structure and civility of talk. Three interventions profiled here include dialogue, fierce conversations, and verbal jujitsu.

Dialogue

The dominant conversational model in the United States relies on discussion as the primary model for discourse. In fact, it might be surprising to discover there is any other type of conversation in our culture! Simply turn on the radio or TV most any time of day and you can find pundits spouting off their opinions with an air of condescension and superiority. Or, walk into any meeting in your organization and listen to people taking turns pushing their agendas, but not really listening to each other. Although blood pressure gets raised during these heated exchanges, little else gets solved. These are discussions. The word *discussion* stems from the Latin *discutere* meaning to "smash to pieces" (Senge et al., 1994, p. 353). The term is also related to the words "percussion" and "concussion" with the general meaning of heaving back and forth to beat the opponent down, and proving a point in a win/lose confrontation. Discussion promotes fragmentation and advocacy wars, but little learning as its participants have dug in their heels, ready to defend their point of view, or else. Discussion plays an important role in helping us decide a course of action, but it can also prevent us from stepping back and truly understanding an issue and the assumptions that lie behind it.

Dialogue is the polar opposite of discussion, and rooted in the Greek roots *dia* (meaning "through" or "with each other") and *logos* (meaning "the word") (Senge et al., 1994, p. 353). Together *dia logos* means "through meaning" (Senge et al., 1994, p. 353). You might think of dialogue as meaning flowing through a group of people. A dialogue helps us understand issues in new ways we've not thought of before. Dialogue can significantly alter the conversational and collective thinking skills of a group to help it garner collective intelligence that exceeds the sum of individual thinking (Senge, Ross, Smith, Roberts, & Kleiner, 1994). A dialogue involves the group in surfacing issues that were previously undiscussable and questioning structures that may be impinging group or organization functioning. As the dialogue unfolds, the knowledge base of the group expands. For example, I worked for years with two groups that competed for resources within a larger institution and did not fully trust the motives of each other. The distrust and competition made it difficult to implement changes in either group's program or to resource allocations. People began to take sides creating divisions between the groups. The members of both groups realized this ongoing conflict was becoming destructive and agreed to explore how it could be resolved. We decided to conduct an action research project to collect data on perceptions between the groups. All group members were interviewed (analysis) and brought together for a feedback session on what the interviews revealed. A series of dialogues (intervention) followed where assumptions about each program were surfaced, along with fears of one group superseding the other. Misperceptions were also surfaced and corrected, going a long way in helping the groups see that it was counterproductive in the larger context of the institution to compete against each other. Both groups were able to create a new vision of working together that has made them stronger, positioning both well for the future to receive resources and support from the larger institution. Energy that used to be devoted to infighting between the groups has now been refocused on building the strength of both groups.

A unique feature of dialogue is that it slows down the speed of conversation by employing deeper levels of reflection and listening (Elinor & Gerard, 1998) and relies on questioning that helps surface individually and collectively held mental models. Getting people to slow down is challenging as most of our organizations thrive on quick action. Yet, dialogue asks us to slow the pace and made a deliberate shift from advocacy-based discussion conversation to inquiry-based dialogical conversation. This means that rather than push my agenda, I must be willing to sit back and understand the agenda of another person and what lies behind it. The goal is not to find the right answer, but rather to examine multiple perspectives surrounding an issue that would not have been possible through individual reflection. Dialogue is the collective engagement in reflective practice with the hope that the collective intelligence of the group will yield better decisions.

Dialogue is founded on respect for divergent viewpoints and designed to be exploratory and open ended so that it does not focus on attaining a predetermined outcome. Dialogue will eventually result in an outcome, but allows the group the leeway to explore important issues that rise to the surface that would otherwise be overlooked and undiscovered in agenda-driven meetings. The primary result of dialogue is a deeper level of understanding and insight that allows for better actions.

Dialogue generates a community-based culture of cooperation and shared leadership. It moves the group from dependency, competition, and exclusion characteristic of hierarchical cultures and increases collaboration, partnership, and inclusion. A nice example is of a general manager of a manufacturing business who was dissatisfied with his one-on-one weekly meetings with direct reports. The meetings yielded fragmented pieces of information that were not helping his executive team work together. He decided to abolish the weekly one-on-one meetings and replace them with a group dialogue with all of his executives on issues in the business. These sessions proved highly effective at creating deeper knowledge about the issues and challenges faced by the business, as well as strengthening the relationships among the participants.

Dialogue is challenging. It requires us to slow down and listen without interrupting. It seeks to surface and interrogate assumptions that are held by group members. It requires a safe environment and willingness to test assumptions. Dialogue skills are useful across many situations and are worth honing both individually and collectively.

Fierce Conversations

"Fierce conversations happen when we come out from behind ourselves into the conversation and make it real" (Scott, 2004, p. 7). They involve taking chances in our conversations that help individuals or groups take large strides toward working on what really matters. Scott articulates four goals of fierce conversations including: interrogate reality, provoke learning, tackle tough challenges, and enrich relationships. Fierce conversations are results-focused and hold participants accountable. The goal is to name and address the issues truthfully and effectively and use the conversation as an impetus for change. Fierce conversations can be confrontational and are aimed at addressing attitudinal, performance, or behavioral issues. Although intended to be respectful, fierce conversations do not necessarily use dialogue as a structuring principle.

During my presidency of a nonprofit organization, I inherited an executive committee of staunch volunteers who had held their officer roles for years. The group was talented and committed, yet none of the members was interested in assuming the presidency of the organization, creating a leadership vacuum. It became clear to me that we needed to develop a new cadre of future leaders by appointing a new executive committee to broaden board members' exposure to leading the foundation. I had to find a way of asking these long-term executive committee members to step down from their positions while keeping them on the board and engaged as stewards of the foundation. I followed Scott's (2004) structure for having a fierce conversation that is outlined below in italics. The fierce confrontation model begins with an opening statement that should take no longer than 60 seconds to make. The opening statement consists of:

1. Naming the issue. *The foundation is weak at cultivating new leaders.*
2. Selecting a specific example that illustrates the behavior or situation you want to change. *The foundation lacks a succession plan and no one on the executive committee is interested in being president.*
3. Describing your emotions about the issue. *I am worried about the future of the organization and also planning to step down from the presidency in another year without a clear successor.*
4. Clarifying what is at stake. *The strong leadership and standing of our organization are at risk without good leadership.*
5. Identifying your contribution to this problem. *I have been a long-term executive committee member and am at fault for not raising this issue earlier even though I know that the Board views our group as insular.*
6. Indicating your wish to resolve the issue. *An important contribution we can all make to the organization is to "fire ourselves" from this role and recruit new people to the task so that we have leaders in the pipeline ready to move into executive positions.*
7. Inviting your partner to respond.

I was nervous about asking these dedicated volunteers to give up their leadership roles, and at this point we opened up the conversation. We moved into the next phase of the fierce conversation model known as the interaction stage. This occurs once you have presented your issue. As each executive committee member responded to my suggestion that we appoint new leadership, it became clear that others harbored similar concerns. The next steps of the model include:

8.   Inquire into your partner's views.
      a. Paraphrase
      b. Seek for full understanding

The final step of the fierce conversation model is resolution and follows the following steps:

9.   Identify what has been learned and what else is needed for resolution and moving forward.
      a. Make a new agreement and determine how you will hold each other accountable for keeping it.

We agreed that I would remain on the executive committee to transition with a new president-elect, along with one other member to help with continuity. We elected new members and now have a strong pipeline of interested and able leaders willing to take over the presidency of the foundation. We also changed our bylaws to clarify the nominating process and selection procedures for the executive committee. The former executive committee members remain engaged in board work and the change has allowed them to contribute in ways they weren't able to due to their previous responsibilities.

Scott (2004) offers some wonderful conversation starters you can use for beginning a fierce conversation. They are listed below.

1.   What is the most important thing we should be talking about today?
2.   What topic are you hoping I won't bring up? What topic am I hoping you won't bring up?
3.   What do we believe is impossible to do, that if we were able to do it would completely change the game? How can we pull it off?
4.   What values do we stand for and are there gaps between those values and how we actually behave?

5. What is our organization pretending not to know? What are we pretending not to know?
6. How have we behaved in ways guaranteed to produce the results with which we're unhappy?
7. What's the most important decision we're facing? What's keeping us from making it?
8. If we were hired to consult to our organization, what advice would we give?
9. If we were competing with our organization, what strategy would we use?
10. If nothing changes, what's likely to happen?
11. What are the conversations out there with our names on them? The ones we've been avoiding for days, weeks, months, years? Who are they with and what are the topics?
12. Given everything we've explored together, what's the next most potent step we need to take? What's going to try to get in our way? When will we take it? When should we touch base about how it went and what's next? (Scott, 2004, pp. 282-283)

Verbal Jujitsu
Verbal jujitsu uses the martial arts principle of channeling a force that is coming toward you and redirecting it to change the situation. In an organization setting, this involves reacting to "undesirable, demeaning statements or actions by turning them into opportunities for change that others will notice" (Meyerson, 2001, p. 96). Pulling off verbal jujitsu requires self-control and emotional intelligence. Meyerson offers the example of a woman whose suggestion is ignored during a meeting and later repeated by a male colleague claiming the idea as his own. In this case, another male interjected to remind the group that they already heard the suggestion from the woman and that it was a good idea worthy of further consideration. Meyerson notes that several things were accomplished by this interaction:

> First, by showing how [the woman] had been silenced and her idea co-opted, he voiced an unspoken fact. Second, by raising [her] visibility, he changed the power dynamic in the room.

Third, his action taught his colleagues a lesson about the way they listened—and didn't. (p. 97)

Verbal jujutsu requires the willingness to take spontaneous risks as opportunities are provided during group interactions.

Opportunistic Interventions

The next category of interventions is based on taking advantage of opportunities to make change when they arise. Making opportunistic interventions requires spontaneity and keen attention to dynamics in the organization. Two interventions will be discussed in this section, including small wins and variable term opportunism.

Small Wins

Using Tom Peter's original description of "small wins" as point of departure, Weick (1984) defines them as "a concrete, complete, implemented outcome of moderate importance" (p. 43). Small wins by themselves may be insignificant but, "A series of wins at small but significant tasks . . . reveals a pattern that may attract allies, deter opponents, and lower resistance to subsequent proposals. Small wins are controllable opportunities that produce visible results" (p. 43). Small wins are fragmented and sought when the opportunity arises in dynamic environments. "Much of the artfulness in working with small wins lies in identifying, gathering, and labeling several small changes that are present but unnoticed" (Weick, 1984, pp. 43-44).

Meyerson (2001) has advocated small wins as a tempered radical strategy. "Small wins . . . give a name to practices and assumptions that are so subtle they are rarely questioned, let alone seen as the root of organizational ineffectiveness" (Meyerson & Fletcher, 2000, p. 135). They are powerful because they help organizations name practices and assumptions that are dysfunctional. "Small wins combine changes in behavior with changes in understanding" (p. 135), and tie the local to the global. Small wins may also be subject to the snowball effect—one small change begetting another to create an altogether new system. Finally small wins aim to fix the organization, not people, freeing stakeholders from anger and blame.

Although Meyerson and Fletcher (2000) advocate finding other like-minded individuals when pursuing small wins, it is not required, and many tempered radicals operate solo by taking localized change and creating more systematic shifts. Meyerson and Fletcher (2000) offer an example of advocate for small wins on issues related to diversity and equity by first diagnosing the problem. This may involve one-on-one interviews or focus groups with stakeholders. They suggest asking questions such as:

* How do people in this organization accomplish their work? What if anything gets in the way?
* Who succeeds in this organization? Who doesn't?
* How and when do we interact with one another? Who participates and who doesn't?
* What kinds of work and work styles are valued in this organization? What kinds are invisible?
* What is expected of leaders in the organization?
* What aspects of individual performance are discussed the most in evaluations? (adapted from Meyerson & Fletcher, 2000, p. 132)

After the initial diagnosis has been made, cultural patterns and their consequences should be identified. Next small wins are designed. This is the process of identifying concrete changes. This may be something as simple as naming an undiscussable dynamic in an organization. In examples from their own work they named meeting overruns, last-minute schedule changes, and tardiness as "unbounded time." "Invisible work" was defined as the work that women often did in the organization. The simple naming of something can have a dramatic effect as it brings a dynamic into the discourse of the organization. They advocate that small wins work so well because they are not random. Rather they "unearth and upend systemic barriers . . ." (p. 134).

Other examples of small wins include (Meyerson, 2001):

* Placing a recycling bin under a desk to encourage recycling.
* Involving cleaning staff to collect and recycle waste.
* Locating a recycling bin in an accessible place (parking lot, common kitchen).

- Using block-out times for meetings (early morning, evening).
- Enlisting other minority hires to hire people from minority groups.
- Naming practices to heighten attention as in the "unbounded time" above.

Positioning to create small wins involves five strategies (Meyerson, 2001).

1. Maintain a "blurry vision." Develop a vision of change that allows for multiple specific outcomes and alternative paths, to create flexibility and allow for opportunism.
2. Create opportunities in the details. Look for opportunities and be ready to act on them.
3. Challenge your sense of organizational tolerance. Use small wins as a way to push existing conventions and constraints outward.
4. Scope and time your challenges wisely. With limited resources, time, credibility, and energy, pick your battles based on timing, scope of impact, probability of success, and so on.
5. Design small wins to generate learning. Think of small wins as experiments that probe conditions and help you and others learn. (p. 110)

Variable-Term Opportunism

Using variable-term opportunism as a critical intervention requires being open to opportunity and jumping on "serendipitous circumstances" (Meyerson, 2001). The short term approach aims to seek "low hanging fruit" that will not create controversy and enlist another in advancing the agenda, and then pointing out the benefits of the change to stakeholders. Meyerson (2001) shares a story of a person who noticed recycling opportunities in his organization and asked the cafeteria manager to make a few moderate changes to be more environmentally sensitive. This small act caused the cafeteria to identify other ways of eliminating waste and resulted in cost savings as well. A longer term example is a woman executive who is hired into a very male, competitive environment, who found the culture to clash with her own leadership style. She decided to run her unit in a style that was entirely counter to the prevailing culture. Although she raised eyebrows at first, it became apparent after a year that her staff was gaining visibility and approving of her leadership, which in turn caused behavioral shifts in her peers in their own management styles.

Learning Interventions

The secret tool adult educators hold is an understanding of learning and change. This knowledge is invaluable as you design and implement interventions since learning and change are inextricably linked. Learning interventions of particular use to critical consultants include reflective practice and critical action technologies.

Reflective Practice

Reflective practice was introduced by Schon (1984) as a process of thinking critically while engaged in practice and on actions taken during practice. It is primarily a process of self-introspection and assessment that has been written about extensively in the adult education literature. Brookfield (1987, citing Boyd & Fales, 1983, p. 100) suggests that reflective learning is closely related to critical thinking, describing it as "the process of internally examining and exploring an issue of concern, triggered by an experience, which creates and clarifies meaning in terms of self, and which results in a changed conceptual perspective" (p. 14). Brookfield points out how critical thinking is used in the workplace practices of strategic planning, effective decision making, creative problem solving, situational leadership, entrepreneurial risk taking, research and development activities, and organizational team building. OD consultants who foster reflective practice on these and other organizational processes will be more effective at helping clients understand the assumptions that underlie their thought and action. Reflective thinking can be encouraged individually, or in group settings through dialogue, discussion, action research, action learning, coaching, mentoring, team building, and planning. Encouraging reflection throughout the action research cycle could be a diagnostic intervention. Reflection can also be integrated into training and development programs that are part of OD interventions. Reflective practice is also imperative for our own growth and development as consultants.

Critical Action Technologies

Action technologies involve a host of collaborative learning tools including the best known action research, action learning, and action science (Brooks & Watkins, 1994). Action technologies' basis in reflective practice and action makes them perfect for critical assessment of organization challenges. Action research is OD's favored data collection model and a critical model is proposed earlier in this book for implementing critical consulting. Action learning is a process of accelerating people's learning about real work problems and/or desired outcomes within the actual work context. It is learning *by doing*, followed by *reflecting on the doing* in a continuous cycle. The outcome of action learning is accelerated learning about real work problems and/or desired outcomes within the actual work context. It involves embracing an issue, raising new questions, reflecting on problems and solutions, making necessary changes, and considering the learning that transpired in the process. I have used action research with a group of women who were struggling with being leaders in male-dominated environments, and nonprofit executive directors who were developing leadership skills with their organizations and boards. In each case, members came together voluntarily to share experiences, mistakes, and questions, and helped each other decide on future courses of action.

Action science is a process of reflecting on a previous encounter, usually a conflict. It requires participants to examine how their actions are often inconsistent with their thoughts. Using a tool called the left-hand column, participants review past interactions by writing what they said in the right-hand column of a worksheet and what they thought or felt on the left-hand column of the worksheet. Inconsistencies are explored. Action science also involves critically reflecting on assumptions held about others or events in the organization. Action science is very effective in resolving conflict and developing functional teams because it helps build authentic communication and examines the contradiction between thought and action. It is also an effective coaching tool when individuals are trying to analyze previous relationships that are problematic and take individual steps to improve them.

In an example of critical action research, Senge et al. (2008) profile how Coca-Cola and the World Wildlife Fund struck an unusual partnership to address the company's water management. This partnership is emblematic of how unlikely partners are joining forces to address issues of sustainability and social justice today. The partnership was in response to the crisis of over 1 billion of the world's population lacking reliable access to safe drinking water. Coca-Cola recognized a responsibility to help the communities solve water problems where it does business. The partners used an action research process to understand perspectives on the issues, starting with asking 250 people throughout the company about their views on water issues and local communities. They followed up with workshops based on the responses of individual facilities, conducting 30 workshops in 6 months and receiving about a 92% response rate from 875 bottling plants around the globe. This OD effort will help address water shortages and provide an example to other companies that use significant amounts of water.

Coalition Building Interventions

OD guru Richard Beckhard once observed, "One person seeking to change an organization will get killed; it doesn't matter what position the person is in. Two can commiserate. Three can become a full-fledged conspiracy" (in Senge et al., 2008, p. 152). The next set of critical interventions examines how to build alliances that will help you implement the desired change. The interventions profiled include networks and strategic alliance building.

Networks

Networking is "the process of contacting and being contacted by people in our social network and maintaining these linkages and relationships...a set of relations, linkages, or ties among people" (Burke, 1993, in Travers, Stevens, & Pemberton, 1997, p. 62) or "the banding together of like-minded people for the purposes of contact and friendship, and support" (Vinnicombe & Colwill, 1996, in Travers et al., p. 62). An informal network is "the set of job-related contacts that a manager relies on for access to task-related, career, and social support" (Ibarra, 1995, p. 674). There are three different types of networks including professional and occupational networks, training networks, and in-company networks (Travers et al., 1997). Keele (1986) defines networks as being composed of weak social ties and used to exchange information and provide support.

Networks can be either informal (i.e., professional associations, personal contacts), or formal and structured entities sponsored by an organization. Networking has been shown to be effective particularly at helping disenfranchised groups in organizations gain voice and power. It is common in organizations today to find groups for women, people of color, and gays and lesbians who organize to advocate on behalf of the group. Networks can serve as an advisory body to their organizations and provide safety in numbers when advocating for policy change that addresses their specific concerns. Although they are often in-company, networks can also be cross-organization. An emerging trend is networks emerging through social networking sites like Facebook and LinkedIn. Creating a network in conjunction with a planned change can be very effective. For instance, during reorganization a network could be formed of women to examine how the new structure might disenfranchise them in terms of new positions or work structures. The network could recommend strategies for retention and development as management plans and implements the changes.

Strategic Alliance Building

Strategic alliance building is a public and collaborative strategy. Banding with other like-minded individuals results in "a sense of legitimacy, access to resources and contacts, technical and task assistance, emotional support, and advice" (Meyerson, 2001, p. 99). Strategic alliance building creates power to illuminate problems and address them with more speed and candor that might have been possible if working alone. Mothers at my institution banded together to pressure the university for better childcare support and options. The collective pressure resulted in quick action from the administration to begin investigating the problem. Meyerson cites the example of a company enlisting senior women and men to explore why women consultants were leaving. It was discovered that the demanding culture of the firm was causing the women to leave, and that the culture was also wearing on the men. So, all parties involved banded together to solve the problem and work to make the culture more balanced.

Meyerson (2001) recommends some tips for organizing collective action:

1. Clarifying the issue and the movement: To galvanize support and inspire action, clarify your purpose by framing the issue broadly, but clearly. Be sure, however, to actively encourage subgoals that reflect the distinct experiences of different participants; doing so helps ensure inclusion and avoid alienation.
2. Internal culture: Focus on the culture of the collective itself, as indicated by norms of behavior, clothing, music, food, language, jokes and so on. Be sure to encompass different identity groups within the collective. Diversity of cultural expression increases the commitment of members whose differences might otherwise preclude alignment.
3. Organizational structure and leadership: Ensure that the collective's leadership and structure do not reflect only a dominant group but a multiplicity of identities and interests.
4. Outside support: Solicit support from people or groups who identify with possible sub-goals as well as the core issues, to create a sensitivity to all constituents relevant to the collective and thus to create a sense of inclusion. (p. 133)

Activism Interventions

As critical consultants we may work from low threat positions where we raise awareness, to high threat positions where we become change activists. This section profiles two activism interventions, disruptive self-expression and tempered radicalism.

Disruptive Self-expression

Disruptive self-expression (Meyerson, 2001) includes subtle acts of private, individual acts that defy the expectations of others.

Examples include personal demonstrations of values, language, dress, office decor, or behavior that begin to change the work atmosphere. Others notice these disruptions and begin to talk about them. Such disruptions may cause others to incorporate their own into their repertoire. For example, I once worked with an executive woman who had an unusual crystal sculpture pin. It was a conversation piece. When people asked her about it, she would explain how it represented the glass ceiling and was her reminder of the necessary work to help women advance. It was her way of starting the conversation about women's issues and a reminder to herself to not take her own success for granted. The more people who talk about the "transgressive act" or replicate it, the greater the change will be. Meyerson cites an example of a manager who refused to schedule late afternoon meetings or take evening calls due to family commitments. His behavior raised concerns about his commitment, but when he met all performance expectations, others begin taking note and modifying the work schedule. Slowly others began adopting the schedule, making the work environment more family friendly for all. Meyerson also cites instances of women asserting their femininity in male-dominated environments through subtle dress, or their racial identity by refusing to remove cornrow braids in the case of an African American consultant.

Tempered Radicalism

The notion of a tempered radical was discussed in Chapter 3, as an important strategy for a critical consultant. This section builds on the information presented there with additional strategies. Meyerson (2001) suggests that tempered radicals make a difference through resisting quietly and staying true to one's "self," turning personal threats into opportunities, broadening the impact through negotiation, leveraging small wins, and organizing collective action. Tempered radicals have to work to not be coopted into the dominant way of thinking. Meyerson offers three strategies for maintaining a positive self-concept and resisting dominant culture's threat to your own identity:

1.   Build relationships with people inside and outside the organi-

zation who share and appreciate marginalized aspects of your identity and can help keep threatened identities alive.

2. Develop a discipline to manage heated emotions to fuel your agenda, which puts you in the driver's seat, and keeps you from giving in to the forces that could marginalize.

3. Separate public "front stage" performance from "backstage" acts to create an appearance of conformity while *acting* on differences to sustain your sense of self (p. 41).

Meyerson offers strategies for turning threatening situations into opportunities drawing on Kolb and Williams's (2000) strategy of the "responsive turn." This strategy "helps you to change the dynamics taking place in [a threatening] encounter. They represent different levels of challenge and varying potential for creating learning" (p. 63).

1. **Interrupt** an encounter to change its momentum. This might happen through stopping someone who is telling a sexist joke by saying, "Do you really want to tell this joke?"

2. **Name** an encounter to make its nature and consequences more transparent. This might mean pointing out that meeting at 7 AM will be a hardship for parents, or that only certain people are receiving development opportunities (typically white male managers).

3. **Correct** an encounter to provide an explanation for what is taking place and to rectify understandings and assumptions. This might happen when a group member is using positional power to foist an action plan on the group. You might intervene by pointing out that no one is willing to disagree with the action plan on the table and invite some alternative suggestions.

4. **Divert** an encounter to take the interaction in a different direction. Change the subject.

5. **Use humor** to release the tension in a situation. Laugh at yourself. Find something humorous to break the tension.

6. **Delay** to find a better time or place to address the issue. Suggest that we are at an impasse and need some time to regroup.

Meyerson also suggests that strategic decisions about how hard to push an agenda must be made considering the following:

1. **Timing:** Is this a good time to take a risk and pose a challenge? Is this a good time for others to be receptive to your idea?
2. **Stakes:** How high are the stakes for the different parties involved in the encounter? Is this a fight worth picking?
3. **Likelihood of success:** How promising are the hoped-for results? Will people learn from the turn? Will they make desired changes in their behaviors?
4. **Options:** Are there better alternative responses to those that would pose a significant risk? Are there responses that will enable you to take a stand without overly jeopardizing your credibility?
5. **Consequences of failure:** What are the worst possible outcomes of the different choices? How bad are they, and how likely are they to occur?
6. **Personal association:** Will this be seen as your "only" issue? Are you outside the interaction or the target of it? If you are the target, would a challenging response be more effective if you could locate a third party to intervene on your behalf?
7. **Doability:** Does a response feel "doable"? Is there a response that is not overwhelming, that you can implement more effectively? (p. 75).

Leading change as a tempered radical requires courage and candor in addressing issues, clarity of purpose, and a creation of a context that helps people feel safe in pursing the goal, similar to a community of learning (Meyerson in Sparks, 2005).

SUMMARY

This chapter focused on the fourth aspect of the framework, the intervention, or structured activities designed to resolve the problem or make the change required in the organization. This chapter defined interventions and set forth criteria for selecting effective interventions. It identified traditional OD interventions. The chapter concluded by offering critical interventions in five categories to include conversational, opportunistic, learning, strategic alliances, and activism. Critical interventions are recommended for consultants who seek to enhance organization well-being, advocate for stakeholders, disrupt the status quo, and create more equitable organizations.

CHAPTER 7

Implementing Representative, Reflective, and Responsible Strategies

This book provided an introduction to implementing a critical approach organization development for human resource developers and adult educators. Instead of taking a rational, neutral stance common in most mainstream OD textbooks, this book described OD as contested and influenced by power and politics. The book recognized that OD knowledge reproduces management and stockholder privilege and argues that this status should no longer go unchallenged, especially by those of us who have committed our work lives to foster organization health and attend to the human side of the organization.

This book defined OD as: *Organization development (OD) is an intentional, systemic process of facilitating change to improve an organization's well-being.* This definition captures the critical action research framework and departs from contemporary definitions and models of OD by shifting the analysis to a more critical level that scrutinizes power relations. The Critical Action Research Model does not assume that all OD practice or its practitioners are inherently logical, rational, or good.

Action research, a widely used framework for OD, is a cyclical process that alternates between action and reflection. Action research is usually participative, enlisting stakeholders in an iterative process of data collection, decision making, implementation, and evaluation. The model in this book added a critical dimension to the action research model, considering diverse stakeholder perspectives including the organization, employees, human resource professionals, adult educators, marginalized groups, and others. This book brought critical reflection to the forefront of OD, sought to strengthen the bridge between adult education and HRD, and tasked you, the OD consultant, with reflecting on your own practice.

The book advanced a framework that shows how OD is influenced by the intersecting interests of the OD consultant, OD stakeholders, OD context, and OD interventions. Although the framework is an artificial representation of multifaceted reality, it helps us understand how the features of OD interact simultaneously as OD issues and interests are negotiated.

As OD consultants, we make up a diverse group of individuals who practice OD and generally use an action research model and a variety of interventions. Those of us who are adult educators may not necessarily regard ourselves as consultants, yet we use OD processes on a regular basis in our work to facilitate learning and change. This book has attempted to identify and label such processes to help adult educators see clearer linkages between their work and that of HRD and OD, and learn how they can use the processes and tools to advance adult education's agenda for social change and justice.

Stakeholders in the OD process are many including not only employees and management, but also clients, customers, and the broader community. Adult education has a long tradition of considering the beneficiaries of its work and seeking social justice. This book has infused that tradition into the consideration of OD stakeholders and challenged OD consultants and organizations to be more socially responsible and sustainable in their work.

The OD context is shaped by dynamic social, political, cultural, economic, technological, and market forces that organizations struggle to respond to. Pressure to perform may result in restructuring, downsizing, and ethical lapses. OD interventions may tend to benefit white male managers over other groups in the organization. In the midst of multiple and sometimes competing pressures, not all stakeholders benefit equally, and management tends to be privileged when organizations undertake change initiatives. Context-sensitive OD helps interpret the political climate and culture, and foreground stakeholders as organizations seek to become more flexible, adaptive, effective, and equitable.

The practice of OD is varied and rich. A wide range of interventions exists to address planned change in organizations through processes such as action research, individual-based strategies including career development and mentoring, group and team-based strategies such as team building and conflict resolution, organization and large-scale-based strategies such as reorganization or vision development, and sociotechnical strategies such as self-managed work teams. Any intervention can be undertaken from a critical perspective. Additionally, this book has offered some new strategies that will be excellent additions to a critical consulting repertoire.

FORGING AN ETHICAL OD PRACTICE

The media and society hold top leaders and financial executives responsible for ethical behavior and point their fingers at them when ethical lapses occur, yet,

> Human resource development professionals are just as guilty and the profession of HRD is as culpable as any CEO or top manager. HRD professionals have been complicit in helping to create organizations and workplaces that do little to enhance the human spirit or protect the environment. (Hatcher, 2002, p. 5)

HRD/OD professionals are fortunate that they have not been arraigned for corruption when major corporations have failed to uphold ethical and moral standards. The HRD/OD profession represents the consciousness of the organization. There is no other function that is charged with representing workers and their needs to management from recruitment to termination of the employment relationship, nor is there one that is so involved with the training, development, and promotion of workers. Yet, there is much work to be done, if OD is to lead organizations to be more ethical and socially responsible (Fenwick & Bierema, 2008; Hatcher, 2002).

Gellerman, Frankel, and Landenson (1990) outline ethical guidelines for OD consultants as *upholding responsibility to ourselves* through acting with integrity and authenticity while seeking self-development and asserting individual interests in a fair and equitable way. We also have a *responsibility for professional development and competence* that means we assume liability for our actions, engage in ongoing learning and development to ensure we are competent professionals, and recognize our own needs and desires with responsibility as we carry out our consulting roles. We have a *responsibility to stakeholders* to serve their long-term well-being and conduct ourselves with honesty, responsibility, and integrity. We have a *responsibility to the profession* to contribute to the knowledge base, promote sharing of knowledge and learning, and respect other OD professionals. Finally, we have a social *responsibility to consider the consequences of our actions* on the client and larger social system, to act with cultural sensitivity, and promote social justice.

CREATING SUSTAINABLE CHANGE

Adult educators and OD consultants are in the change business. We want the changes we have worked so hard to facilitate to be lasting and effective. Burke (2008) summarizes eight factors that promote successful change:

1. Securing top-management support.
2. Building on the unique strengths and values of the organization.
3. Involving all levels of the organization in specifying the plans for change.
4. Creating holistic change that respects the system.
5. Planning change through a process of involved education of all employees.
6. Implementing changes in authority and power relations to support implementation.
7. Approaching change from a stakeholder standpoint.
8. Adapting to change as an ongoing process.

These are important recommendations for sustaining change, yet they are not enough for reinforcing critical change. We must serve as activists who are willing to ask tough questions and raise undiscussable issues, particularly related to equity. When we must oversee difficult changes, such as downsizing, it is important that such activities be conducted with respect and preservation of dignity. No one wants to supervise unfortunate events such as job loss.

OD consultants, however, are uniquely positioned to pose alternative solutions to job loss, and when there is no other option, advocate for affected workers by lobbying for compensation and benefits and respectful treatment. We must also actively assess the results of our efforts to see who is benefiting, and make adjustments when OD interventions create unintended consequences or harm. These actions will move us closer to a truly critical OD theory and practice.

IMPLEMENTING CRITICAL OD THEORY AND PRACTICE

The work to challenge dominant theories and practices of OD is ongoing. Gephart, Thatchenkery, and Boje (1996) offer strategies for reconstructing organizations. This can be accomplished by challenging modernist paradigms of organization development and attempts to impose rationality and neutrality into the process. Another strategy is adopting a "discourse of intense reflexivity" (p. 360) by engaging in deep reflection about OD thought and action, applying strategies forwarded by Argyris and Schon (1974, 1978). We must also continue reconstructing organizations and challenging traditional theories of structure, technology, environment, and effectiveness. Finally, we need to challenge notions of "organizational effectiveness" referred to as "an ideological tool of management control in modernism (Gephart et al., 1996, p. 362) and develop theories and practices that are anti-performative.

Just as we work to challenge dominant management thought and practice, so too must the work continue to develop a critical OD practice. Reynolds (1999) and Trehan, Rigg, and Steward (2007) offer guidance in this regard:

- Question the assumptions and unspoken beliefs underlying both theory and practice.
- Bring to the foreground power issues and the ideology subsumed within the social context of organization structures, procedures, and practices.
- Confront claims of rationality and objectivity by revealing the vested interests they conceal.

- Work toward an emancipatory, antioppression ideal of just organizations and a just society.

These actions and principles will move us closer to a critical OD in the future.

OD IN THE FUTURE

The framework presented in this book represents a critical and holistic way forward as OD shapes itself for the 21st century into a representative, relevant, reflective, and responsible process. What will OD look like in the years to come? Cummings and Worley (2005) predict that it will become more embedded in organizations' operations and rely more on technology. They also expect the OD process to become faster and more interdisciplinary, and serve a broader range of organizations including small business, government, and nonprofit. They also predict that OD will become more cross-cultural and concerned with ecological sustainability.

I agree with Cummings and Worley's (2005) predictions, but do not think they go far enough in challenging OD to become a leader in creating sustainable, ethical, healthy organizations, and developing theories and practices that advance this work. I predict that OD will develop a more critical stream that infuses mindful and activist practice committed to responsible and emancipatory social change. I agree with Cummings and Worley (2005) and McLean (2006) that OD will become more reliant on technology and virtual practices. I predict that the action research process will become computer mediated if not virtual and that several OD interventions will be virtual such as mentoring, coaching, training, action learning, management development, and strategic planning. My vision is for a representative OD—one that critically evaluates who benefits, tends to all stakeholders, respects diversity, and provides relevant interventions that improve work lives and organizations. A reflective OD is imperative—one that engenders ongoing critical assessment and development. Finally, I envision a responsible OD—one that plays an active and leadership role in creating sustainable, humane, antioppression organizations.

REFERENCES

Academy of Human Resource Development. (1999). *Standards for Ethics and Integrity.*

Acar, W., Aupperle, K. E., & Lowy, R. M. (2001). An empirical exploration of measures of social responsibility across the spectrum of organizational types. *The International Journal of Organizational Analysis, 9*(1), 26-57.

Ackerman, L. S. (1997). Development, transition or transformation: The question of change in organizations. In D. F. Van Eynde, J. C. Hoy, & D. C. Van Eynde (Eds.), *Organization development classics: The practice and theory of change—The best of the OD Practitioner.* San Francisco: Jossey-Bass, 45-58.

Ackoff, R. L. (1974). *Redesigning the future.* New York: Wiley.

ACLU (American Civil Liberties Union). *The rights of immigrants: No. 20.* Retrieved June 1, 2002, from http://www.aclu.org/library/pbp20.html Fall 1997l.

Allen, K. R., & Baber, K. M. (1992). Ethical and epistemological tensions in applying a postmodern perspective to feminist research. *Psychology of Women Quarterly, 16,* 1-15.

Alvesson, M. (1996). *Communication, power and organization.* Berlin/New York: deGruyter.

Alvesson, M., & Deetz, S. (2000). *Doing critical management research.* London: Sage.

Alvesson, M., & Deetz, S. (2005). Critical theory and postmodernism: Approaches to organizational studies. In C. Grey & H. Willmott (Eds.), *Critical management studies: A reader*, pp. 60-106. Oxford, England: Oxford University Press.

Alvesson, M., & Willmott, H. (Eds.). (1992). Critical management studies. *London: Sage.*

Alvesson, M., & Willmott, H. (1996). *Making sense of management: A critical introduction.* London: Sage.

Alvesson, M., & Willmott, H. (2003). *Studying management critically.* London: Sage.

Argyris, C. (1964). *Integrating the individual and the organization.* New York: Wiley.

Argyris, C. (1970). *Intervention theory and method: A behavioral science view.* Reading, MA: Addison Wesley Publishing.

Argyris, C. (1973). *On organizations of the future.* Beery Hills, CA: Sage Publications.

Argyris, C. (2000). Intervention theory and method. In W. L. French, C. H. Bell, & R. A. Zawacki (Eds.), *Organization development and transformation: Managing effective change* (5th ed.). Boston: McGraw-Hill, pp. 117-121.

Argyris, C., Putnam, R., & Smith, D. M. (1985). *Action science: Concepts, methods, and skills for research intervention.* San Francisco: Jossey-Bass.

Argyris, C., & Schon, D. A. (1974). *Theory in practice: Increasing professional effectiveness.* San Francisco: Jossey-Bass.

Argyris, C., & Schon, D. A. (1978). *Organizational learning.* Reading, MA: Addison-Wesley.

Asch, S. (1952). *Social psychology.* New York: Prentice-Hall.

Axelrod, R. (1992). Getting everyone involved: How one organization involved its employees, supervisors, and managers in redesigning the organization. *Journal of Applied Behavioral Science, 28*(4).

Axelrod, R.. (1993). Using the conference model TM for work redesign. *Journal for Quality and Participation*, December 1993, pp. 58-61.

Axelrod, R. (1995). The conference model TM approach. *Perspectives* (a newsletter of the Axelrod Group). Wilmette, IL: The Axelrod Group.

Baba, M. L. (1986). *Business and industrial anthropology: An overview.* (Report No. 86-26602). Washington, DC: National Association for the Practice of Anthropology.

Barlow, M., & Robertson, H. (1996). Homogenization of education. In J. Mander & E. Goldsmith (Eds.), *The case against the global economy and for a turn toward the local.* San Francisco: Sierra Club Books.

Basgen, B., & Blunden, A. *Encyclopedia of Marxism.* Retrieved July 13, 2004, from http://www.marxists.org/glossary/index.htm

Beckhard, R. (1967, March-April). The confrontation meeting. *Harvard Business Review, 45,* 149-155.

Beckhard, R. (1969). *Organization development: Strategies and models.* Reading, MA: Addison-Wesley.

Beckhard, R. (1997). Who needs us? Some hard thoughts about a moving target—the future. In D. F. Van Eynde, J. C. Hoy, & D. C. Van Eynde (Eds.), *Organization development classics: The practice and theory of change—The best of the* OD Practitioner. San Francisco: Jossey-Bass, 11-25.

Beckhard, R., & Harris, R. (1987). Organizational transitions. Reading, MA: Addison-Wesley.

Beer, M. (1980). *Organization change and development.* Santa Monica, CA: Goodyear Publishing.

Bennett, G. F. (2001). Religious diversity in the workplace: An emerging issue. *The Diversity Factor,* 15-20.

Bennis, W. G. (1969). *Organization development: Its nature, origins and prospects.* Reading, MA: Addison-Wesley.

Bennis, W. G., Benne, K. D., & Chin. R. (Eds.). (1961). *The planning of change.* London: Holt, Rinehart & Winston.

Betts, F. (1992). How systems thinking applies to education. *Educational Leadership, 50,* 3, 38-41.

Bierema. L. L. (1996). Development of the individual leads to more productive workplaces. In R. Rowden (Ed.), *Workplace learning: Debating the five critical questions of theory and practice,* New Directions for Adult and Continuing Development, No. 72, 21-28. San Francisco: Jossey-Bass.

Bierema, L. L. (1996, Spring). Total quality and adult education: A natural partnership in the classroom. *Innovative Higher Education, 20*(3):145-169.

Bierema, L. L. (2001). Women, work and learning. In T. Fenwick (Ed.), *Sociocultural perspectives on learning through work.* New Directions for Adult and Continuing Education, No. 92, 53-62. San Francisco: Jossey-Bass.

Bierema, L. L. (2002). The sociocultural contexts of learning in the workplace. In M. V. Alfred (Ed.), Learning in sociocultural contexts: Implications for adult, community, and workplace education. New Directions for Adult and Continuing Education, No. 96, 69-78. San Francisco: Jossey-Bass.

Bierema, L.. L. (2002). A feminist approach to HRD research. *Human Resource Development Review, 1*(2), 244-267.

Bierema, L. L. (In Press). Adult learning in the workplace. In J. M. Dirkx (Ed.), *Adult learning and the emotional self.* New Directions for Adult and Continuing Education, San Francisco: Jossey-Bass.

Bierema, L. L., & Cseh, M. (2003). Evaluating HRD research using a feminist research framework. *Human Resource Development Quarterly, 14*(1), 5-26.

Bierema, L. L., & D'Abundo, M. L. (2004). HRD with a conscience: Practising socially responsible HRD. *International Journal of Lifelong Education, 23*(5), 443-458.

Bierema, L. L., & Fenwick, T. J. (2005). Defining critical human resource development. *Proceedings of the Academy of Human Resource Development,* Colorado.

Billett, S. (2001). Co-participation: Affordance and engagement at work. In T. Fenwick (Ed.), *Sociocultural perspectives on learning through work*. New Directions for Adult and Continuing Education, No. 92, San Francisco: Jossey-Bass.

Blake, R., & Mouton, J. (1964). *The managerial grid*. Houston: Gulf

Blake, R. B., & Mouton, J. S. (1976). *Consultation*. Reading, MA: Addison-Wesley.

Blake, R. R., & Mouton, J. S. (1983). *Consultation: A handbook for individual and organization development*. Wokingham: Addison-Wesley.

Block, P. (1981). *Flawless consulting: Guide for getting your expertise used*. Austin: Learning Concepts.

Block, P. (1999). *Flawless consulting: A guide to getting your expertise used*. 2nd ed. New York: Pfeiffer.

Bohman, J. (1996). Critical theory and democracy. In D. Rasmussen (Ed.), *The handbook of critical theory*. Oxford: Blackwell, 190-215.

Boyd, E. M., & Fales, A. W. (1983). Reflective learning: Key to learning from experience. *Journal of Humanistic Psychology, 23*(2), 99-117.

Bradford, D. L., & Burke, W. W. (2004). Introduction: Is OD in crisis? *The Journal of Applied Behavioral Science, 40*(4), 369-373.

Bradford, P. (1999). Workplace learning: Developing an holistic model. *The Learning Organization, 6* (1), 18-29.

Brand, K. B. (1989). *Business ethics in the Netherlands*. Het: Spectrum.

Brookfield, S. D. (1987). *Developing critical thinkers: Challenging adults to explore alternative ways of thinking and acting*. Milton Keynes, Open University Press.

Brookfield, S. D. (1990). *The skillful teacher*. San Francisco: Jossey-Bass.

Brooks, A., & Watkins, K. (1994). *The emerging power of action inquiry technologies*. New Directions for Adult and Continuing Education, No. 63. San Francisco: Jossey Bass.

Brounstein, M. (2001). *Communicating effectively for dummies*. New York: Wiley.

Bruhn, J. G. (2001). *Trust and the health of organizations*. New York: Kluwer Academic/Plenum Publishers.

Bunker, B., & Alban, B. (1992). What makes large group interventions effective? *Journal of Applied Behavioral Science, 28*(4).

Bunker, B. B., Alban, B. T., & Lewicki, R. J. (2004). Ideas in currency and OD practice: Has the well gone dry? *The Journal of Applied Behavioral Science, 40*(4), 403-422.

Burke, W. (1993). Networking. In N. Nicholson (Ed.). *Encyclopedic dictionary of organizational behavior*. Oxford: Blackwell.

Burke, W., & Hornstein, H. A. (1972). *The social technology of organization development*. Fairfax, VA: Learning Resources Corp.

Burke, W. W. (1992). *Organization development: A process of learning and changing* (2nd ed.). Reading, MA: Addisson-Wesley.

Burke, W. W. (2008). *Organization change: Theory and practice* (2nd ed.). Thousand Oaks, CA: Sage.

Burn, S. M. (2004). *Groups: Theory and practice.* Belmont, CA: Thompson Wadsworth.

Business Impact. (2000). Winning with integrity: A guide to social responsibility. *Business in the Community.* London.

Caffarella, R., & Merriam, S. B. (2000). *Linking the individual learner to the context of adult learning.* In A. L. Wilson & E. R. Hayes (Eds.), *Handbook of adult and continuing education.* San Francisco: Jossey-Bass.

Cameron, K., Freeman, S., & Mishra, A. (1991). Best practices in white-collar downsizing: Managing contradictions. *Academy of Management Executive, 5,* 62.

Carr, A. (2000). Critical theory and the management of change in organizations. *Journal of Organizational Change Management, 13*(3), 208-220.

Carroll, A. B. (1999). Corporate social responsibility: Evolution of a definitional construct. *Business & Society, 38,* 268-295.

Catalyst. (2007). Catalyst releases 2006 census of women in Fortune 500 corporate officer and board positions. Retrieved September 15, 2008, from http://www.catalyst.org/press-release/60/catalyst-releases-2006-census--of-women-in-fortune-500-corporate-officer-and-board-positions

Catalyst. (2007). Damned or doomed: Catalyst study on gender stereotyping at work uncovers double-bind dilemmas for women. Retrieved September 19, 2008, from http://www.catalyst.org/press-release/71/damned-or-doomed-catalyst-study-on-gender-stereotyping-at-work-uncovers-double-bind-dilemmas-for-women

Catalyst. (2008). Higher number of women in the boardroom heralds future increase of women corporate officers, according to latest Catalyst study. Retrieved on 6-15-09 from http://www.diversityjournal.com/articles/WBD-WCO_Correlation_press_release.pdf

Cavanagh, M. M., & Prasad, A. (1996). Critical theory and management education: Some strategies for the critical classroom. In R. French and C. Grey (Eds.), *Rethinking management education,* pp. 76-93. London: Sage.

Cervero, R. M., & Wilson, A. L. (2001). *Power in practice: Adult education and the struggle for knowledge and power in society.* San Francisco: Jossey-Bass.

Cervero, R., & Wilson, A. (2005). *Working the planning table: Negotiating democratically for adult, continuing and workplace education.* San Francisco: Jossey-Bass.

Clarkson, M. B. E. (1995). A stakeholder framework for analyzing and evaluating corporate social performance. *Academy of Management Review, 24,* 92-117.

Clegg, S., & Dunkerley, D. (2005). Critical issues in organizations. In C. Grey & H. Willmott (Eds.), *Critical management studies: A reader*, pp. 46-59. Oxford, England: Oxford University Press.

Clifford, J., & Marcus, G. E. (Eds.). *Writing culture: The poetics and politics of ethnography.* Berkley: University of California Press.

Cockman, P., Evans, B., & Reynolds, P. (1996). *Client-centered consulting: Getting your expertise used when you're not in charge.* New York: McGraw-Hill.

Cooper, T., & Kulisa, J. (2003). Critical pedagogy and teaching management in university: Examining the possibilities and limitations. *Proceedings of the 3rd International Critical Management Studies Conference,* July 7-9. Lancaster, England.

Cooperrider, D. L., Barrett, F., & Srivastva, S. (1995). *Social construction and appreciative inquiry: A journey in organizational theory.* Ashgate Publishing: In- Management and Organization: Relational Alternatives to Individualism.

Corson, D. (2000). Emancipatory leadership. *International Journal of Leadership in Education: Theory and Practice, (3)* 2, 93-120.

Covaleski, M. A., Dirsmith, M. W., Heian, J. B., & Samuel, S. (1998). The calculated and the avowed: Techniques of discipline and struggles over identity in big six public accounting firms. *Administrative Science Quarterly, 43,* 293-327.

Coyner, S. (1988-1989). Feminist theory in research and teaching. *National Women's Studies Association Journal, 1,* 290-296.

CRO: Corporate Responsibility Officer. (1997). Member notes: Highlighting CRO members' corporate responsibility initiatives. *CRO: Corporate Responsibility Officer, 2*(1), 64.

Crosby, F. (1999). The developing literature on developmental relationships. In A. J. Murrell, F. J. Crosby, & R. J. Ely (Eds.), *Mentoring dilemmas: Developmental relationships within multicultural organizations,* pp. 3-20. Mahwah, NJ: Lawrence Erlbaum Associates.

Crosby, P. (1979). *Quality is free.* New York: McGraw-Hill.

Cummings, T. G. (2007). *Handbook of organization development.* Thousand Oaks, CA: Sage.

Cummings, T. G., & Worley, C. G. (1993). *Organization development and change,* 5th ed. St. Paul, MN: West Publishing.

Cummings, T. G., & Worley, C. G., (2005). *Organization development and change,* 8th ed. Mason, OH: Thompson-Southwestern.

Dannemiller, K., & Jacobs, R. (1992). Changing the way organizations change: A revolution of common sense. *Journal of Applied Behavioral Science, 28*(4).

Dannemiller, K., et al. (1994). *Consultant guide to large-scale meetings*. Ann Arbor: Dannemiller-Tyson Associates.

Davis, J. R., & Davis, A. B., (1998). *Effective training strategies: Comprehensive guide to maximizing learning in organizations*. San Francisco: Berrett-Koehler.

Deetz, S., & Kersten, A. (1983). Critical models of interpretive research. In L. Putnam, & M. Pacanowsky (Eds.), *Communication and organizations*. Beverly Hills: Sage.

Deming, W. E. (1982). *Quality, productivity, and competitive position*. Cambridge: MIT Press.

Deming, W. E. (1986). *Out of crisis*. Cambridge: MIT Press.

Digh, P. (1998). Race matters. *Mosaics: Society of Human Resource Development, 4*(5), 1, 4-6.

Digh, P. (1999). Can't anyone here speak English?" *Mosaics: Society of Human Resource Development, 1999, 4*(6), 1, 4-7.

Digh, P. (1999, July/August). In and out of the corporate closet. *Mosaics: Society of Human Resource Development, 5*(4), 1, 5-7.

Drucker, P. F. (1974). *Management: Tasks, responsibilities, practices*. New York: Harper & Row.

EEOC (Equal Employment Opportunity Commission). (March 11, 2009). Religion-based charges FY 1992 - FY 2001. Retrieved from http://www.eeoc.gov/stats/religion.html

Ellinor, L., & Gerard, G. (1998). *Dialogue: Creating and sustaining collaborative partnerships at work*. New York: John Wiley & Sons.

Elliott, C., & Turnbull, S. (2002). *Critical thinking in HRD—A panel led discussion*. In T. Marshall Egan & S. Lynham (Eds.). *Proceedings of the 2002 Academy of Human Resource Development Conference*. Honolulu, Hawaii.

Fagiano, D. (1996, June 5). *The legacy of downsizing*. Management Review.

Farmer, H. S., & Associates. (1997). *Diversity and women's career development: From adolescence to adulthood*. Thousand Oaks, CA: Sage.

Fast Company. (2007). The HIP scorecard: A new way of looking at the human side of investment performance. *Fast Company, 114,* 84-85. http://www.fastcompany.com/articles/2007/03/companies-that-care.html

Fenwick, T. J. (2000). Putting meaning into workplace learning. In A. Wilson & E. Hayes (Eds.), *Handbook* (pp. 294-311). San Francisco: Jossey-Bass.

Fenwick, T. (2001). Tides of change: New themes and questions in workplace learning. In T. Fenwick (Ed.), *Sociocultural perspectives on learning through work*. New Directions for Adult and Continuing Education, No. 92. San Francisco: Jossey-Bass.

Fenwick, T. (2003, July 7-9). Ethical dilemmas of transformative pedagogy in critical management education. *Proceedings of the 3rd International Critical Management Studies Conference*. Lancaster, England.

Fenwick, T. J. (2004). Towards a critical HRD in theory and practice. *Adult Education Quarterly, 54*(3), 193-210.

Fenwick, T., & Bierema, L. L. (2008). Corporate social responsibility: Issues for HRD engagement. *International Journal of Training and Development, 12*(1), 24-35.

Forester, J. (1989). *Planning in the face of power*. Berkeley: University of California Press.

Foucault, M. (1979). *Discipline and punish*. Harmondsworth: Penguin.

Freeman, R. E. (1984). *Strategic management: A stakeholder approach*. Boston: Pitman.

French, W., Bell, C., & Zawacki, R. (2000). *Organization development and transformation: Managing effective change*. New York: McGraw-Hill/Irwin.

French, W. L., & Bell, C. H. (1999). *Organization development: Behavioral science interventions for organization improvement*. 6th ed. Upper Saddle River, NJ: Prentice Hall.

Friedman, M. (1962). *Capitalism and freedom*. Chicago: University of Chicago Press.

Galbraith, J. (2006). Matching strategy and structure. In J. V. Gallos (Ed.), *Organization development: A Jossey-Bass reader* (pp. 565-582). San Francisco: Jossey-Bass.

Gallos, J. V. (Ed.). (2006). *Organization development: A Jossey-Bass reader*. San Francisco: Jossey-Bass.

Garvin, D. A. (1988). *Managing quality, the strategic and competitive edge*. New York: The Free Press.

Gee, J. P., Hull, G., & Lankshear, C. (1996). *The new work order: Behind the language of the new capitalism*. Boulder: Westview Press.

Gellerman, M., Frankel, M. S., & Ladenson, R. F. (1990). *Values and ethics in organization and human systems development: Responding to the dilemmas in professional life*. San Francisco: Jossey-Bass.

Goldberg, A., & Ritter, B. (Writers). (2006). Costco CEO finds pro-worker means profitability: High wages, employee benefits build loyalty — and P.R. ambassadors [Television series episode]. In *20/20*. New York: American Broadcasting Company. Retrieved April 18, 2009, from http://abcnews.go.com/2020/business/story?id=1362779

Goldman Schuyler, K. (2004a). The possibility of healthy organizations: Toward a new framework for organizational theory and practice. *Journal
of Applied Sociology/Sociological Practice, 21*(2)/ *6*(2), 57-79.

Goldman Schuyler, K. (2004b). Practitioner—Heal thyself! Challenges in en-
abling organizational health. *Organization Management Journal—
Emerging Scholarship, 1*(1), 28-37.

Graig, L., Haley, J., Luss, R., & Schieber, S. J. (2002). The perfect (demographic)
storm: The impact of a maturing workforce on benefit costs. *Compensation & Benefits Management, 18*(1), 16-26.

Greenhaus, J. H., Parasuraman, S., & Wormley, W. M. (1990). Effects of race on
organizational experiences, job performance evaluations, and career
outcomes. *Academy of Management Journal, 33*(1), 64-86.

Greiner, L. E., & Cummings, T. G. (2004). Wanted: OD more alive than dead.
The Journal of Applied Behavioral Science, 40(4), 374-391.

Grey, C., & Willmott, H. (Eds.). (2005). *Critical management studies: A reader.*
Oxford, England: Oxford University Press.

Grey, C., & Willmott, H. (Eds.). (2005). In C. Grey & H. Willmott (Eds.). Introduction. *Critical management studies: A reader* (pp. 1-15). Oxford, England: Oxford University Press.

Grey, C., & French, R. (1996). Is a critical pedagogy of management possible?
In R. French & C. Grey (Eds.), *Rethinking management education* (pp.1-
16). London: Sage .

Hackett, G., & Byars, A. M. (1996) Social cognitive theory and the career
development of African American women. *The Career Development
Quarterly, 44*(4), 322-334.

Hackman, J. R., & Goldman, G. R. (1980). *Work redesign.* Reading, MA:
Addisson-Wesley.

Hale, J. (1998). *The performance consultant's fieldbook: Tools and techniques
for improving organizations and people.* San Francisco: Jossey-Bass.

Hammer, M., & Champy, J. (1993). *Reengineering the corporation: A manifesto for business revolution.* New York: HarperCollins.

Hancock, P., & Tyler, M. (2001). *Work, postmodernism and organization: A
critical introduction.* London: Sage.

Hanscome, L., & Cervero, R. M. (2003).The impact of gendered power relations in HRD. *Human Resource Development International, 6*(4), 509-
525.

Hatcher, T. (2002). *Ethics and HRD: A new approach to leading responsible
organizations.* Cambridge, MA: Perseus Publishing.

Heesun, W. (2002, April 11). Corporate ethics: Right makes might. *Business Week*. Retrieved, June 24, 2004, from http://www.businessweek.com/ bwdaily/dnflash/apr2002/nf20020411_6350.htm http:/www.heidisloss. com/growth-spurts/2008/9/5/women-corporate-board-count-a-new-benchmark-for-profitabilit.html

Helgesen, S. (1990). *The female advantage: Women's ways of leadership*. New York: Doubleday.

Hinkley, R. C. (2002). How corporate law inhibits social responsibility. *Humanist, 62*(2), 26-28.

Hofstede, G. (1986). Editorial: The usefulness of the organizational culture concept. *Journal of Management Studies, 23*(3), 253-257.

Hoque, F. (2007). Corporate social responsibility: Using a humanitarian business model. *CRO: Corporate Responsibility Officer, 2*(6), 45-46.

Humble, J. (1975). *The responsible multinational enterprise*. London: Foundation for Business Responsibilities.

Hyatt, J. C. (2008). CRO trends. *CRO: Corporate Responsibility Officer, 3*(2), 11.

Ibarra, H. (1995). Race, opportunity, and diversity of social circles in managerial networks. *Academy of Management Journal, 38*(3), 673-703.

International Labour Organization (ILO). (2007). Global employment trends for women 2007. Retrieved, August 20, 2008, from http://www.ilo.org/ public/english/region/ampro/cinterfor/temas/gender/news/gl_tren.htm

Johnson-Bailey, J., & Cervero, R. M. (2000). The invisible politics of race in adult education. In A. L. Wilson & E. R. Hayes (Eds.), *Handbook of adult and continuing education* (New ed., pp.147-160). San Francisco: Jossey-Bass.

Juran, J. (1974). *Quality control handbook* (3rd ed.). New York: McGraw-Hill.

Katz, D., & Kahn, R. L. (1978). *The social psychology of organizations* (2nd ed.). New York: Wiley.

Keele, R. (1986). Mentoring or networking? Strong and weak ties in career development. In L. L. Moore (Ed.), *Not as far as you think*. Lexington, MA: Lexington Books.

Kellner, D. (1995). *Media culture: Cultural studies, identity, and politics between the modern and the postmodern*. New York and London: Routledge.

Kincheloe, J. L. (1999). *How do we tell the workers? The socioeconomic foundations of work and vocational education*. Boulder, CO: Westview Press/ Perseus.

Kok, P., van der Wiele, T., McKenna, R., & Brown, A. (2001). A corporate social responsibility audit within a quality management framework. *Journal of Business Ethics, 31*, 285-297.

Kolb, D. A. (1981). Learning styles and disciplinary differences. In A.W. Chickering & Others (Eds.), *The modern American college.* San Francisco: Jossey Bass.

Kolb, D. A. (2000). *Facilitator's guide to learning.* Hay/McBer: David A. Kolb Experience-based Learning Systems, Inc.

Kolb, D., & Williams, J. (2000). *The shadow negotiation.* New York: Simon and Schuster.

Korten, D. C. (1995). *When corporations rule the world.* San Francisco: Berrett-Koehler.

Korten, D. C. (1996, March) *When corporations rule the world.* Paper presented at the meeting of the Academy of Human Resource Development Conference. Minneapolis, MN.

Korten, D. C. (1998). *Globalizing civil society: Reclaiming our right to power.* New York: Seven Stories Press.

Kram, K. E. (1985). *Mentoring at work.* Glenview, IL: Scott, Foresman.

Kuchinke, K. P. (1999) Adult development towards what end? A philosophical analysis of the concept as reflected in the research, theory, and practice of human resource development. *Adult Education Quarterly, 49*(4), 148-162.

Lach, J. (1999). Minority women hit a concrete ceiling. *American Demographics, 21*(9), 18-19.

LaMotta, L. (2007). Caring, the corporate way. *Fast Company.com.* Retrieved, August 15, 2008.

Lawler, E. E. (1982). Increasing worker involvement to enhance organizational effectiveness: Design features for participation systems. In P. S. Goodman & Associates (Eds.). *Change in organizations.* San Francisco: Jossey-Bass.

Lawler, E. E. (n.d.). Designing high-performance organizations. Retrieved February 5, 2005, from http://unpan1.un.org/intradoc/groups/public/documents/un/unpan001316.pdf

Lawrence, J. (1991). Action learning—a questioning approach. In A. Mumford (Ed.), *Gower handbook of management development*(3rd ed.), pp. 241-247. Aldershot, Hans: Gower.

Lawson, K. (2006). *The trainer's handbook* (2nd ed.). San Francisco: Pfeiffer.

Lee, D. (2007). Human resources: Diversifying the religious experience. *CRO: Corporate Responsibility Officer, 2*(6), 40-41.

Lewin, K. (1947). Quasi-stationary social equilibria and the problem of permanent change. In W. G. Bennis, K. D. Benne, & R. Chin (Eds.) (1961) *The planning of change.* London: Holt, Rinehart & Winston.

Lewin, K. (1948). *Resolving solving social conflicts: Selected papers in group dynamics.* New York: Harper & Brothers.

Lippitt, R., & Lippitt, G. (1975). Consulting process in action. *Training and Development Journal, 29*(5), 48-54; *29*(6) 38-44.

Lippitt, R. J., Watson, J., & Westley, B. (1958). *Dynamics of planned change.* New York: Harcourt, Brace.

Little, J. S., & Triest, R. K. (2002, First Quarter). The impact of demographic change on labor markets. *New England Economic Review,* 47-68.

Lockwood, N. R. (2004, Dec.). Corporate social responsibility: HR's leadership role. *HR Magazine.* Retrieved August 2, 2008, from http://findarticles. com/p/articles/mi_m3495/is_12_49/ai_n8583189

Maher, F. A., & Tetreault, M. K. T. (1994). *The feminist classroom: A look at how professors and students are transforming higher education for a diverse society.* New York: Basic Books.

Malik, K. (2001, Spring). The perils of pluralism: A re-examination of the terms of engagement between races and cultures, and a plea for equality. *The Diversity Factor,* 31-34.

Marsick, V. J. (1997). Reflections on developing a code of integrity in HRD. *Human Resource Development Quarterly, 8(2), 91-94.*

Martin, J. (2003). Feminist theory and critical theory: Unexplored synergies. In M. Alvesson & S. Deetz (Eds.), *Studying management critically* (pp. 66-91). London: Sage.

Martin, R. J., & Van Gunten, D. M. (2002). Reflected identities: Applying positionality and multicultural social reconstructionism in teacher education. *Journal of Teacher Education, 53*(1), 44-54.

Maurer, T. J., & Rafuse, N. E. (2001). Learning not litigating: Managing employee development and avoiding claims of age discrimination. *Academy of Management Executive, 15*(4), 110-121.

McDaniel, R. R., & Walls, M. E. (1997). Diversity as a management strategy for organizations: A view through the lenses of chaos and quantum theories. *Journal of Management Inquiry, 6*(4), 363-375.

McGregor, D. (1960). *The human side of the enterprise.* New York: McGraw-Hill.

McLean, G. N. (2006). *Organization development: Principles, processes, performance.* San Francisco: Berrett-Koehler

McLean, G. N., Sytsma, M., & Kerwin-Ryberg, K. (1995, March). Using 360-degree feedback to evaluate management development: New data, new insights. In E. F. Holton III (Ed.), *Academy of Human Resource Development 1995 Conference Proceedings* (Section 4-4). Austin, TX: Academy of Human Resource Development.

Merron, K. (2006). Masterful consulting. In J. V. Gallos (Ed.), *Organization development: A Jossey-Bass reader* (pp. 365-384). San Francisco: Jossey-Bass.

Meyerson, D. (2001). *Tempered radicals: How people use difference to inspire change at work.* Boston: Harvard Business School Press.

Meyerson, D. E. (2001, October). Radical change, the quiet way. *Harvard Business Review,* 92-100.

Meyerson, D. E. (Fall 2004). The tempered radicals: How employees push their companies—little by little—to be more socially responsible. *Stanford Social Innovation Review,* 14-23.

Meyerson, D. E., & Fletcher, J. K. (2000, January-February). A modest manifesto for shattering the glass ceiling. *Harvard Business Review,* 127-136.

Meyerson, D. E., & Scully, M. A. (1995). Tempered radicalism and the politics of ambivalence and change. *Organization Science, 6*(5), 585-600.

Miller, R. A. (1998). Lifesizing in an era of downsizing: An ethical quandary. *Journal of Business Ethics, 17,* 1693-1700.

Mirvis, P. H. (2006). Revolutions in OD: The new, and the new, new things. In J. V. Gallos (Ed.), *Organization development: A Jossey-Bass reader* (pp. 39-88). San Francisco: Jossey-Bass.

Moir, L. (2001). What do we mean by corporate social responsibility? *Corporate Governance, 1*(2), 16-21.

Monaghan, C. H. (2003, July 7-9). Silence, voice, and resistance in management education. *Proceedings of the 3rd International Critical Management Studies Conference.* Lancaster, England, pp. 303-317.

Morgan, G. (1996). *Images of organization* (2nd ed.). San Francisco: Sage.

Morris, B. (2006, July 11). New rule: Agile is best; being big can bite you. Old rule: Big dogs own the street. *Fortune. Retrieved, July 15, 2006, from* http://money.cnn.com/2006/07/10/magazines/fortune/rule1.fortune/index.htm

Nadler, L., & Nadler, Z. (1989). *Developing human resources: Concepts and a model* (3rd ed.). San Francisco, CA: Jossey-Bass.

Niles, S. G., & Harris-Bowlsbey, J. (2004). *Career development interventions for the 21st century* (2nd ed.). Upper Saddle River, NJ: Prentice Hall.

Nocera, J. (2008, May 24-25). Parting words of an airline pioneer. *International Herald Tribune,* 15-16.

Owen, H. (1992). *Open space technology: A user's guide.* Potomac, MD: Abbott.

Parker, G. M. (2006). What makes a team effective or ineffective? In J. V. Gallos (Ed.), *Organization development: A Jossey-Bass reader* (pp. 656-680). San Francisco: Jossey-Bass.

Pasquariello, A. C. (2007). Grant makers. *Fast Company, 114,* 32.

Porras, J. I. & Bradford, D. L. (2004). A historical view of the future of OD: An interview with Jerry Porras. *The Journal of Applied Behavioral Science, 40*(4), 392-402.

Porras, J. I., & Robertson, P. J. (1992). Organizational development: Theory, practice, and research. In M. D. Dunnette, & L. M. Hough (Eds.), *Handbook of industrial and organizational psychology*, (2ⁿᵈ ed., vol. 2.) Palo Alto, CA: Consulting Psychologists Press.

Porter, J. L., Muller, H. J., & Rehder, R. R. (1989). The making of managers: An American perspective. *Journal of General Management, 14,* 62-76.

Preston, H. H. (2008, May 24-25). A tighter link between ethics and share prices. *International Herald Tribune,* 19.

Quigley, B. A. (1997). The role of research in the practice of adult education. In B. A. Quigley & G. W. Kuhne (Eds.), *Creating practical knowledge through action research: Posing problems, solving problems, and improving daily practice.* New Directions for Adult and Continuing Education, No. 73. San Francisco: Jossey-Bass.

Rapoport, R., Bailyn, L., Fletcher, J. K., & Pruitt, B. H. (2002). *Beyond work-family balance: Advancing gender equity and workplace performance.* San Francisco: Jossey-Bass.

Ray, M., & Rinzler, A. (Eds.). (1993). *The new paradigm in business: Emerging strategies for leadership and organizational change.* New York: G. P. Putnam.

Revans, R. W. (1980). *Action learning—New techniques for managers.* London: Blond and Briggs.

Reynolds, M. (1999). Grasping the nettle: Possibilities and pitfalls of critical management pedagogy. *British Journal of Management, 9,* 171-184.

Rice, J. (2007). Diversifying the management team. *CRO: Corporate Responsibility Officer, 2* (2), 43-44.

Rigg, C., & Trehan, K. (1999). Not critical enough? Black women raise challenges for critical management learning. *Gender and Education, 11*(3), 265-280.

Rio, T. G., & Sanders-Reio, J. (1999). Combating workplace ageism. *Adult Learning, 11*(1), 10-13.

Roberts, A. (2000). Mentoring revisited: A phenomenological reading of the literature. *Mentoring & Tutoring, 8*(2), 145-170.

Rosseau, D. M. (1995). *Psychological contracts in organizations: Understanding written and unwritten agreements.* Thousand Oaks: Sage.

Ross-Smith, A., & Kornberger, M. (2004). Gendered rationality? A genealogical exploration of the philosophical and sociological conceptions of rationality, masculinity and organization. *Gender, Work & Organization, 11*(3), 280-305.

Rubin, J. Z., Pruitt, D. G., & Kim, S. H. (1994). *Social conflict: Escalation, stalemate, and settlement* (2ⁿᵈ ed.). New York: McGraw-Hill.

Russo, A. R. (2001). Observations on corporate citizenship. *The CPA Journal, 71*(9), 12.

Sacks, D. (2007). Working with the enemy. *Fast Company, 188,* 74-81.

Sambrook, S. (2003, July 7-9). A 'critical' time for HRD? *Proceedings of the 3rd International Critical Management Studies Conference.* Lancaster, England.

Schall, D. (2007). CRO 10: CRO's 10 best corporate citizens by industry, 2007. *CRO: Corporate Responsibility Officer, 2*(6), 24-33.

Schein, E. H. (1987). *Process consultation, Vol. 2: Lessons for managers and consultants.* Reading, MA: Addison-Wesley.

Schein, E. H. (1988). *Process consultation, Vol. 1: Its role in organization development* (2nd ed.). Reading, MA: Addison-Wesley.

Schmuck, R., & Miles, M. (1971). *Organization development in schools.* Palo Alto, CA: National Press Books.

Schon, D. (1984). *The reflective practitioner: How professionals think in action.* New York: Basic Books.

Schrieber, P. J.(1998). Women's career development patterns. In L. L. Bierema (Ed.), *Women's career development across the lifespan: Insights, and strategies for women, organizations, and adult educators.* New Directions for Adult and Continuing Education, No. 80. San Francisco: Jossey-Bass.

Schulz, A. (2007). 100 best corporate citizens 2007. *CRO: Corporate Responsibility Officer, 2*(1), 20-28.

Senge, P., Ross, R., Smith, B., Roberts, C., & Kleiner, A. (1994). *The fifth discipline fieldbook.* New York: Currency Doubleday.

Senge, P., Smith, B., Kruschwitz, N., Laur, J., & Schley, S. (2008). *The necessary revolution: How individuals and organizations are working together to create a sustainable world.* New York: Doubleday.

Senge, P. M. (1990). *The fifth discipline: The art and practice of the learning organization.* New York: Doubleday/Currency.

SHRM, Society of Human Resource Management. (2001). What is the 'business case' for diversity? Retrieved, 06-15-09 from http://www.shrm.org/diversity/default.asp?page=businesscase.htm

Simpson, W. G., & Kohers, T. (2002). The link between corporate social and financial performance: Evidence from the banking industry. *Journal of Business Ethics, 35,* 97-109.

Slawson, D. (1998, May). Information mastery: Feeling good about not knowing everything. Keynote address at the 1998 Family Practice Research Day. Michigan State University. East Lansing, MI.

Slawson, D., Shaughnessy, A., Ebell, M., & Barry, H. (Eds.). (1997). *Evidence-based practice: Patient-oriented evidence that matters.* Stamford: Appleton & Lange.

Slawson, D., Shaughnessy, A., Ebell, M., & Barry, H. (Eds.). (1997). *Evidence-based medicine use with acute sinusitis, educational programs to prevent back injuries, or screening for depression.* Stamford: Appleton & Lange.

Smith, J., & Smith, J. (1994). Notes from ASTD Future Search Conference. Southern Minnesota Section, American Society for Training and Development: Apple Valley, MN.

Sparks, D. (2005). Tempered radicals speak courageously to inspire change. *National Staff Development Council, 26*(1), 20-23.

Spencer, B. (2001). Challenging questions of workplace learning researchers. In T. Fenwick, (Ed.) *Sociocultural perspectives on learning through work.* New Directions for Adult and Continuing Education. No. 92. San Francisco: Jossey-Bass.

Stahl, M. J., & Grigsby, D. W. (1997). *Strategic management; total quality & global competition.* Oxford: Blackwell.

Stone, C. D. (1975). *Where the law ends: The social control of corporate behavior.* Prospect Heights, IL: Waveland Press.

Suchman, M. C. (1995). Managing legitimacy: Strategic and institutional approaches. *Academy of Management Review, 20,* 571-610.

Swanson, D. L. (1995). Addressing a theoretical problem by reorienting the corporate social performance model. *Academy of Management Review, 20,* 43-64.

Swanson, R. A., & Holton, E. F. (2001). *Foundations of human resource development.* San Francisco: Berrett-Koehler.

Thomas, K. M. (2005). *Diversity dynamics in the workplace.* Belmont, CA: Thompson Wadsworth.

Tisdell, E. J. (1995). Creating inclusive adult learning environments: Insights from multicultural education and feminist pedagogy, Information series No. 361. Columbus, OH: ERIC Clearing House on Adult, Career and Vocational Education.

Tisdell, E. J. (2001). The politics of positionality: Teaching for social change in higher education. In R. M. Cervero & A. L. Wilson (Eds.), *Power in practice: Adult education and the struggle for knowledge and power in society* (pp. 145-163). San Francisco: Jossey-Bass.

Training. (1997, October). 1997 Industry Report. *Training,* 33-75.

Travers, C., Stevens, S., & Pemberton, C. (1997). Women's networking across boundaries: Recognizing different cultural agendas. *Women in Management Review, 12*(2), 61-70.

Trehan, K., Rigg, C., & Stewart, J. (2007). Going beyond a critical turn: Hypocrasies and contradictions. In C. Rigg, J. Stewart, & K. Trehan (Eds.), *Critical human resource development: Beyond orthodoxy* (pp. 239-249). Essex, England: Prentice Hall.

Tripp, D. (1991). Critical theory and educational research. *Issues in Educational Research, 2*(1), 13-23.

U.S. Census Bureau. (2000) *Population estimates program.* Population Division. Washington, DC.

U.S. Census Bureau. (2001). *200 years of U.S. census taking: Population and housing questions 1790-1990.* U.S. Department of Commerce: U.S. Bureau of the Census. Washington, DC: Available from AmeriStat Website. http://www.ameristat.org/racethnic/census.htm

U.S. Department of Labor. (2006). Employed persons by detailed occupation and sex, 2006 annual averages. Retrieved, August 1, 2008), from http://www.bls.gov/cps/wlf-table11-2007.pdf

U.S. Department of Labor Women's Bureau (U.S. DoL). (1994). Facts on working women: Women of Hispanic origin in the workforce. " Retrieved, 06-15-09 from http://www.dol.gov/dol/wb/public/wb_pubs/hisp931.htm

U.S. Immigration and Naturalization Service. (1999). Legal immigration, Fiscal year 1998. *Statistics Branch Annual Report,* Washington, DC.

Vaill, P. B. (1989). Seven process frontiers for organization development. In W. Sikes, A. B. Drexler, & J. Gant (Eds.), *The emerging practice of organization development* (p. 261). La Jolla, CA: Co-published by NTL Institute and University Associates.

Valentin, C. (2003, July 7-9). How can I teach critical management in this place? Contradictions and compromise on a multi-cultural masters programme in HRD: A study of work in progress. *Proceedings of the 3rd International Critical Management Studies Conference.* Lancaster, England.

VanBuren, J. J. (2000). The bindingness of social and psychological contracts: Toward a theory of social responsibility in downsizing. *Journal of Business Ethics, 25,* 205-219.

VanBuren, M. & Erskine, W. (2003) *The 2002 state of the industry report.* Alexandria, VA: American Society for Training and Development.

Verschoor, C. C. (1998). A study of the link between a corporation's financial performance and its commitment of ethics. *Journal of Business Ethics, 17*(13), 1509-1517.

Vince, R. (2003, July 7-9). Towards a critical practice of HRD. *Proceedings of the 3rd International Critical Management Studies Conference.* Lancaster, England.

Vinnicombe, S. & Colwill, N. L. (1996). *The essence of women in management.* Engelwood Cliffs, NJ: Prentice-Hall.

Waclawski, J., & Church, A. H. (Eds.). (2002). *Organization development: A data-driven approach to organization* change. San Francisco: Jossey-Bass.

Wagner, C. (2001, July-August). Evaluating good corporate citizenship. *The Futurist*, 16.

Wartick, S. L., & Wood, D. J. (1998). *International business and society.* Malden: Blackwell Publishers.

Weick, K. E. (1984). Small wins: Redefining the scale of social problems. *American Psychologist, 39*(1), 40-49.

Weisbord, M. (1992). *Discovering common ground.* San Francisco: Berrett-Koehler.

Weisbord, M., & Janoff, S. (1995). *Future search — An action guide to finding common ground in organizations & communities.* San Francisco: Berrett-Koehler.

Wheatley, M. (1992) . *Leadership and the new science: Learning about organization from an orderly universe* (Chapter 7). San Francisco: Berrett-Koehler.

Wheatley, M., Tannenbaum, R., Yardley, P., Griffin, P., & Quade, K. (2003). *Organization development at work: Conversations on the values, applications and future of OD.* San Francisco: Pfeiffer.

Willmott, H. (1993). Breaking the paradigm mentality. *Organization Studies, 14*(5), 681-720.

Willmott, H. (1997). Critical management learning. In M. Burgoyne & M. Reynolds (Eds.), *Management learning.* London: Sage.

Wirtenberg, J., Abrams, A., & Ott, C. (2004). Assessing the field of organization development. *Journal of Applied Behavioral Science, 40*(4), 465-479.

Wood, D. J. (1991). Corporate social performance revisited. *Academy of Management Review, 16,* 691-718.

Worell, J. (1991). Progress and prospect. *Psychology of Women Quarterly, 15,* 1-6.

Worell, J. (1996). Opening doors to feminist research. *Psychology of Women Quarterly, 20,* 469-485.

Worell, J., & Etaugh, C. (1994). Transforming theory and research with women. *Psychology of Women Quarterly, 18,* 443-450.

Worley, C., & Feyerherm, A. (2003). Reflections on the future of OD. *Journal of Applied Behavioral Science, 39,* 97-115.

Zinn, L. M. (1991). Identifying your philosophical orientation. In M. W. Galbraith (Ed.), *Adult learning methods* (pp. 39-77). Malabar, FL: Krieger.

INDEX